"Packed with insightful suggestions and superb ideas for service opportunities all around us."

Stephen R. Covey
Author of *The 7 Habits of Highly Effective People*
and *The 8th Habit: From Effectiveness to Greatness*

This book is a great resource for two types of people: those who want to provide service but simply don't know how, and those who have grand intentions but can't muster the energy to achieve their goals and end up doing nothing.

Lynette Rasmussen, director
Office of Work and Family Life
Department of Workforce Services, Salt Lake City, Utah

In a hedonistic world, this is a must-read if we are ever to break through the self-centered society we find ourselves caught up in. This book is the best cure for depression! Terri's book takes the fear out of service. She shows us by real-life examples the many types of situations that sufferers may face and the possibilities for service they present. In a day full of "movement," Terri has taught me that service starts with making room to quiet down, contemplate, and start listening to the daily promptings that, when acted upon, bring me a joy I would have missed before reading this book.

Robbie Lawler
National Young Mother of the Year, 1995

I meet hundreds of people each week, and so many of them, each successful and talented in his or her own way, share the same loss of direction when it comes to the basic "how tos" of extending human kindness. It is a disheartening and embarrassing problem for many of us who want to do more. Terri beautifully shares a highly individualized yet unifying path in *So, You're Not Mother Teresa*. In a wonderful few moments of bright, witty, and touching reading, you will have your answers as I did.

Kim Powers
Founder, Grapevine Radio, Healthy Wealthy Wow

So, you're not
MOTHER TERESA

So, you're not MOTHER TERESA

A Detailed "How Can I Help? " Resource
For Giving Random Acts Of Kindness

Terri Minus

TATE PUBLISHING & Enterprises

Published by Tate Publishing & Enterprises, LLC
127 E. Trade Center Terrace | Mustang, Oklahoma 73064 USA
1.888.361.9473 | www.tatepublishing.com

Tate Publishing is committed to excellence in the publishing industry. The company reflects the philosophy established by the founders, based on Psalm 68:11,
"The Lord gave the word and great was the company of those who published it."

Book design copyright © 2009 by Tate Publishing, LLC. All rights reserved.
Cover design by Jonathan Lindsey
Interior design by Janae J. Glass

Published in the United States of America

ISBN: 978-1-60696-976-2
1. Reference: Personal & Practical Guides
2. Family & Relationships: General
09.01.06

To those loved ones who believe in me

Acknowledgments

This book is a result of a collaborative effort. There were many anonymous contributors to the extensive lists of suggestions, and I appreciate their cooperation and generosity in sharing their ideas. Without their input there would be about four ideas from which to choose.

My girlfriends have been the backbone of support during this project, beginning with Tayna, who has always been my number-one cheerleader. She has been the constant friend factor and buoyed me during our walks and soul-to-soul talks. Darlene, who has an intuitive perspective that I have come to trust, which allows me to have faith in myself and hope for the future. Stephanie, who has believed in me for over twenty-five years and always offers wit and wisdom, which transforms our conversations into laughing fests. Roxanne, my aunt, who has become more like a sister to me over the years, has cheered me on and been supportive in important ways.

Family is my foundation. During this long process of

creating a finished product, my children were patient and gave the space and time to do the necessary work. I thank my sweet and tender daughter, Avery, who has taught me much about loving service in the midst of personal heart-ache. She was very encouraging and supportive when I began this journey and has continued to express her interest in this project. I tip my hat to my two sons, who are amaz-ing people and have loving and giving hearts. I have learned much from watching them serve others so willingly. My son Dane introduced me to the joy of unbounded love for another human being because he was my firstborn, and his gentle, loving, and sensitive nature is easy to be around. My son Collin loves deeply in a quiet way. He has always been appreciative of the things I have done for him, which makes my heart swell with increased tenderness toward him.

My mother, Judy, has been a great example of sharing gifts from her heart all her life. Her loving service to others over the years has softened her and increased her divine con-nection. She is well loved by many people. She is constant in her support for my happiness and wise in her counsel.

I particularly want to acknowledge my beloved husband, Christopher. He has been unfailingly encouraging, support-ive, and patient during my moments of doubt and discour-agement. I especially thank him for how he conducts his life. He lives in integrity and honor with a soul that naturally generates numerous acts of kindness, even if it results in an inconvenience to himself. His example is consistent, humble, and pure. It always fuels in me a desire to give of myself in the same way and inspires me to live at a higher standard than my natural inclinations.

Table of Contents

Introduction

Many people in the world, like me, struggle with giving service and acts of kindness. It is not a question of being there for family and friends. That comes naturally and willingly. My lack is in giving aid and assistance to the next layer of individuals beyond my familiar comfort level. When an opportunity to serve becomes apparent, my reaction is like a deer caught in headlights. I mentally freeze up, feel a little confused, and let the opportunity pass me by. I think and think and come up with nothing more than giving a plate of cookies. The cookie dough is always ready. But there are many circumstances for which a plate of cookies simply isn't appropriate. Now what? With no idea of what to do, original or not, I lose interest in the desire to help, and the immediate opportunity is gone. In a day or two I feel a pang of guilt and self-recrimination. However, the guilt doesn't inspire action on my part, and the window of opportunity to help closes as I mentally march forward in my list of things to do for the day.

My mother thinks she has failed me. However, she is a great example of knowing how to serve others and thinking of their needs then acting on it. For years, I have observed her quietly and lovingly contribute acts of kindness, as she is able. Despite her example, since my early youth I have always felt the lack of knowing what to do in a situation where loving acts from the heart would help. I was always aware that this never came easy to me. With the immaturity and insecurity of youth, I did little or nothing to develop a desire to serve others beyond my comfort zone.

As I have continued to mature, it has become obvious to me, that my inability to be service-minded must change. In a world with frequent catastrophes large and small that require more help than can be handled at a government level, it has become necessary for all people to reach out and perpetuate acts of compassion and kindness that will help reduce stress-filled life situations. It is essential for all of us to develop awareness of others' needs and then follow through with specific action.

The world as we know it seems to be experiencing diverse catastrophic events with increasing frequency. The tsunami in Indonesia, relentless hurricanes in the Gulf States, the endless wars in the Middle East, earthquakes the world over, especially in the Far East, India, and Pakistan, terrorism at home and abroad, wars throughout the world, famines, out-of-control diseases, raging forest fires, droughts in one season and fearsome blizzards and storms in another season, all contributing to large-scale human suffering beyond what can be imagined. The resulting cries for help from the affected communities and the people whose lives are disrupted are overwhelming. It is heartrending to see such suffering. I am confident in stating that life on this earth will continue to experience these kinds of disasters. The need to answer the call to serve our fellow human beings is clear. Because of the increasing amount of disasters, I believe we must prepare ourselves for more personal involvement in the future and begin to contribute more of our compassionate energies now.

There are many opportunities all around. The problem for me was knowing specifically what to do. I looked for a book that would give me ideas and suggestions to get me started. What I found were many books that encouraged the reader to get involved and make a difference but seldom offered specific ideas. The lists of suggestions were minimal and common. I would watch talk shows that highlighted peoples' needs here in America and around the world. After an hour of information and high-energy encouragement, I would feel a great desire to do something. I read many articles addressing the same theme: help the needy and the broken-hearted. Again, I would feel a great desire to contribute something of my time and efforts to help someone in need. However, I found simplistic suggestions and with my own lack of imagination I was stumped. It was so frustrating for me to feel my lack of ideas. At this point, I thought I couldn't be the only one "out there" who needed direction. I decided to begin gathering information from people I knew, or people I was referred to, who understood and followed through with how to ease the heartaches of tender and difficult life situations. So a book was born.

While researching the material for this book, I observed and interviewed many compassionate, kindhearted people.

I found they shared common traits. For the most part, these people exuded a loving, gentle, and generous quality in their interactions with others. There was a nonjudgmental essence about them, which fostered a sense of feeling emotionally and physically safe in their company. A mature and loving radiance emanated from them. They are the kind of individuals who draw others to them. People naturally want to be around this kind of person.

I believe the people I observed in action are a microcosm of what is played out in thousands of communities around the world. These communities are filled with similarly kind-hearted, other-centered individuals who contribute compassionate acts of service to ease the pain, distress, and suffering of their neighbors. Remember, we don't need to fly to the ends of the earth to help. We can make a difference to the people in our own neighborhoods or communities. The needs are just as great and just as significant in our own backyard.

Chapters 6 and 7 are the soul of this book. These sections are filled with specific ideas and suggestions for service. Chapter 6—"Creative Ideas of a General Kind(ness)"—is filled with ideas that can be used in many types of circumstances. The ideas are just that, general. Chapter 7—"Do Something! Specific Ideas for Specific Situations"—categorizes twenty-seven different topics of needs or situations that are common among people everywhere. Following the topics are listed multiple suggestions that can facilitate service specifically tailored to that need.

A friend of mine experienced a serious fall that resulted in a long recuperation period. She did not want anyone offering gifts, service, or visits. However, one woman did bring her a "girl movie" and some chocolates. I thought it a clever idea because I relish chocolate, and sometimes there is nothing like a good movie to make me feel better. So I have frequently recommended taking a chocolate treat and a good movie with you in addition to anything else you are offering.

The message within these pages is offered with hope for a change of willingness, attitude, and ability to give of your time, means, and talents. The ideas are basic and the suggestions simple. My intention is not to overwhelm you on any level. It is a place to start. This book is written especially for those who have difficulty knowing what to do and where to start but want very much to help. I tip my hat to those who have already figured it out.

In doing the research for this book, I felt it was most authentic to interview people I had observed, personally knew, or who were referred to me by someone who felt I must talk with their acquaintance. There are dozens of people who have contributed to the bulk of the suggestions listed in Chapters 6 and 7. I must mention that almost 100 percent of the people I interviewed were reluctant to offer their insights and experiences because their acts of kindnesses are given from their hearts. They are completely uninterested in getting recognition for these gifts of love. Therefore, in order for me to draw from their wealth of experiences, I reassured them I would not use their real names in reference to their experiences or suggestions. The book is peppered with real examples of kindness from people whose names I have changed.

Chapter 1

Joy in the Soul

Joy is prayer—Joy is strength—Joy is love—Joy is a net of love by which you can catch souls. She gives most who gives with joy. Joy is love, the normal result of a heart burning with love. Joy is a need and a physical power. Our lamp will be burning with sacrifices made out of love if we have joy. The best way to show our gratitude to God and the people is to accept everything with joy. A joyful heart is the inevitable result of a heart burning with love.

—Mother Teresa[1]

A few years ago as I was driving home from a birthday massage, I was in a contemplative state of mind. I began to ruminate on the inward journey I was actively pursuing. I was giving time and attention to processes and activities that assisted in clearing out toxic history and old belief patterns and programs that had been weighing me down over the years. I reflected on how much I had taken care of, how clear I was feeling, and what a lot of hard work was accomplished. It was a long and difficult road, but I had made tremendous progress. All of a sudden I blurted out, "She's back!" I realized in that moment the true essence of my soul had reemerged. I recognized the sensation immediately. It was joy!

Due to unfortunate circumstances in my childhood, I had carefully and gently layered my soul's divine joy with a protective shroud. I taught myself to withdraw emotionally from life on a very deep level. Instinctively I detached emotionally to protect my joyful core from being destroyed. As a child I didn't have the awareness or understanding that I could express my confusion and pain. I stayed quiet. The resulting emotional state, however, was forty years of subtle depression that blocked my ability to be fully engaged in life at a more genuine joyful level. The brown, murky energy laying on me was a constant state of being. It was not obvious to outsiders. It was lurking just under the emotional radar screen. It was easy to mask, easy to smile over. But it did affect the quality of my life immensely. I just wasn't aware of it because I was detached.

Until that poignant moment on the freeway, I knew I was off center, but I could not identify why I was off center. Some years ago I felt my soul getting restless. As I began to pay attention to the message this restlessness was sending me, I knew I had some inner house cleaning to tackle. I started the journey of healing that would uncover layer by layer the shroud I had carefully woven to protect my joyful center. That freeway experience marked the moment when it was safe enough for me to allow my eight-year-old girl's joy to return. What a wonderful moment that was for me!

I am vigilant now in maintaining that joyfulness. I know that it is a state of being to which each person is born. We are joyous, joy-filled, and joy-intended beings! As we grow from infancy to adulthood, we encounter life's onslaught of negative and painful experiences. They come at us in a myriad of ways and chip away at our natural joyfulness. A few lucky ones somehow maintain a fuller sense of joy, while others lose it entirely. The masses of humanity grope through life, trying to reclaim it, not really even knowing what "it" is. "It" is joy in the soul. Joy at the core and center of the human being. It is an integral and basic substance of our souls.

As the poem that Mother Teresa penned indicates, joy is an eternal state of being that connects us with God. It is a spiritual place inside of us. To retain that joy, she writes of ways to cultivate it daily—loving, helping, giving, serving, rescuing, and living in the present moment. Each of these verbs when applied to our lives contributes to retaining that soul filled with joy, which is our natural state.

An accumulation of more and more things of the world will never satiate this longing to connect with our core and our spiritual essence and nature. Things break, rust, get old, get lost, change, and are forgotten. If you actively and consciously feed and nourish another's joy, your own joy will never break, rust, get old, get lost, or be forgotten. You may be sad, lonely, disappointed, frustrated, angry, or upset, but you can still hold onto your sense of joy, for that is who you are. It may get buried under the pain because of life's circumstances, but it still defines your nature.

This book is about how to nourish your joy by serving others. It is not about putting yourself into a place of servitude that gives other people power over you. Willingly serving others is the foremost ingredient in a diet of maintaining joy in the soul. This service can be difficult, inconvenient, time consuming, and sometimes heartbreaking. But given with loving intention, your vessel of joy will be fortified. You will be changed. You will be softened. You will develop a grace and radiance and light about you that will draw others to you. They may not know what it is about you that they are attracted to, but it will be the joyful core of your soul that emanates from within.

A friend of mine said, "Most enlightened people know they need to serve." Albert Schweitzer said it this way: "Just do what you can. It's not enough merely to exist...you must do something more. Seek always to do some good, somewhere." He continues in expressing his opinion that for each person to realize her own nobility and true worth, she must give time and offerings of help, "for which you get no pay, but the privilege of doing it."[2]

Serving becomes a contagious experience. The more you serve others, the more you want to serve. Today's world is hungry for people who serve. When you are seen acting in kindness toward others, it gives others courage to do the same. Pass it on, pay it forward, and perpetuate goodness. Simple gifts from the heart and acts of charity have immeasurable repercussions for spreading emotional relief and fortifying faith in the goodness of our fellow man.

Chapter 2

Receiving Is Giving

There is an old adage that states, "It is better to give than to receive." This is true if one is promoting the morality of selflessness in a world filled with people who perpetuate the philosophy and lifestyle of "It's all about me." (Oh, kind of like the world in which we now live!) However, there is an opposite but complementary view, which is seldom thought of that, when examined and understood, creates a full and complete principle of higher living.

Miriam learned this lesson while recovering from back surgery. She had consistently felt very reluctant to accept anyone's help during frequent physical challenges. Miriam was taught as a child, "We'll do it ourselves." She passed that same training on as she raised her three boys. They were capable of taking care of their own! This lifelong philosophy created in her a sense of capability in maintaining self-reliance under any of her life's circumstances, and she was hesitant to interrupt other people's time and schedules or to feel needy. She would turn down people's offers to help, while believing she was doing the right thing. As she continued healing from her surgery, one day Miriam received a very distinct impression that she was being selfish. In this moment of enlightenment, she was taught that her selfishness denied someone else the opportunity to serve her and give of themselves. She learned she was not allowing these people to grow from their giving. She was also denying them the chance to receive the blessings that flow from compassionate service.

For the most part, we want to retain our independence and self-reliance no matter what age we are or in what circumstances we live. We have been taught to be strong individualists. Any appearance of needing help is regarded as a weakness or a lack of ability to be in control of our lives. Heaven forbid we might need something from someone.

I read an article by Wally Amos about this topic of giving and receiving. He concluded his thoughts with, "Giving *is* receiving." It caught me off guard. I processed the thought for a moment or two and realized that he was right. The giver is rendering help and assistance. By doing so the giver is learning the pure joy that comes from stepping outside themselves. Equally important, while the receiver is benefiting from the gifts that are given, she is allowing the giver to receive an opportunity for growth.

Giving and receiving are partners, each with equal importance. Each of us at some time on our journey through this life will be in a position to receive service from others, as well as give service to someone else. Being in a position of receptivity is often induced by circumstances not of our choosing; therefore, we feel vulnerable and powerless. This opens us up to being dependent on factors outside of our control. It's emotionally uncomfortable. When we are in the position of giving service we feel more comfortable. This is because we are in control of our actions. But sometimes we don't have a choice. It's one of life's funny ways of teaching us about opposition.

However, each part, receiving and giving, is an opposite side of the same coin. They both have equal merit and value. Miriam taught me on that day of our interview: "If you don't have a receiver, you can't be a giver." It is important for us to remember the dignity and magnificence of each part.

The following story illustrates one man's understanding of this principle. The giver in this story also taught the observers a great lesson about the dignity and joy of service.

> A committee of prominent Chicago citizens waited in one of the city's railroad stations. They were to welcome one of the greatest men in the world. He arrived and greeted them in three languages. He was a giant of a man, six feet four inches tall with bushy hair and a walrus mustache. The reception committee stood, talking about how honored they were to meet him and how the important people of the city were waiting to entertain him. Reporters took down his every word. Flash cameras were busy taking his picture.
>
> Suddenly the giant of a man asked to be excused. He walked rapidly through the crowd onto the station platform.

Coming to an old woman who was struggling with heavy suitcases, he scooped up her bags with his great hands. Then he told her to follow him. He worked his way through the throng and took the woman to her coach. After wishing her a good journey, he returned to the committee.

"Sorry to have kept you waiting, gentlemen," he said to the astonished group. "I was just having my daily fun."

The distinguished visitor was Albert Schweitzer, famous philosopher-musician-doctor-missionary.

"First time I ever saw a sermon walking," said one of the reporters. A member of the reception committee remarked, "A lot of us stuffed shirts were unstuffed that moment." Well they might be. A man with a world mission, engaged in writing a profound history of civilization, was demonstrating, in a simple, unaffected way, the love of God for the least individual, and the democracy of true brotherhood. [3]

The "very important people of the city" received two lessons that day.

One, giving service can be a satisfying and joyful experience. Two, even "important" people can emulate this humble approach to life and have fun while doing it. From age thirty until the end of his life at age ninety, Dr. Schweitzer was devoted to serving all living creatures. It is inspirational to read about his loving attitude toward his life's work. He was unwaveringly committed to service. He displayed an uplifting and contagious attitude of joyfulness about giving of himself to others, whether high or lowborn.

Present-Moment Living

This story also sheds light on another important concept that Dr. Schweitzer exhibited. It is the ability to live in the present moment, being fully engaged in what is happening now. Even when surrounded by the press and important people, he was present enough to notice an elderly woman struggling with her luggage and obviously in need of assistance. He exemplified the necessity of being alive in the now and not allowing life's distractions to chase away an opportunity to alleviate another human being's suffering.

In recent years "stay in the present moment" has become a very popular catch phrase. This focused attention and attitude of being is touted with increased frequency in many self-help books, spiritual guidebooks, and physical-training books, but it is an age-old concept. It is one of the core philosophies of the ancient yogis. In our fast-paced world, we have been taught that happiness or fulfillment or bigger and better is just around the corner. Because of this attitude, we have a tendency to focus on what is supposedly coming to us instead of what is already in front of us. When we live in constant anticipation for greater things to come, we lose out on the fullness of our lives in the present. It's a huge disservice to the quality of our todays.

Children throughout time and cultures display in perfect innocence a natural-born ability to stay present. When you observe children in their play or interaction with life, they are fully engaged in what is directly in front of them. Their focus and concentration is pure. "Pay attention! Look at me! Are you listening?" are all phrases that we use to pull children away from this total concentration and focus. Obviously, there are justifiable reasons for our need to get their attention. However, to illustrate the point of staying present, consider a child's ability to be completely absorbed in the present moment. If we can recapture that ability to be in the now (because we were all children once upon a time), we will reap richer and more satisfying benefits from every activity in which we are engaged. Applying the principle of present-moment living when we engage in giving acts of kindness is essential to being truly effective.

Mother Teresa understood this principle with her philosophy of serving "one, one, one." Serving the one is all she wanted to do, because she knew that serving one individual at a time was the most effective way to help.

"I never look at the masses as my responsibility," she said. "I look only at the individual. I can love only one person at a time. I can feed only one person at a time. Just one, one, one."[4] Staying present with the one you are assisting and serving gives power to the experience and changes lives.

To be truly effective in our service we must be mentally present. It is embarrassing when you are giving of your time and talents to people and they catch you in disinterest. It's a nice thing you offer, but when they sense your heart or mind isn't with them, they recognize you have diminished their importance in lieu of something else that has caught your attention. In their eyes the sincerity of your love and your motivation to serve them is questioned. You have compromised your integrity. Stay focused. Stay present. Let them feel they are the most important person in your life at that moment. It is vital they know that the service you give them has your full, undivided attention. Be as the small child. Stay enthusiastically engaged and focused.

Miriam continues to be plagued with physical infirmities. Her attitude is wonderful in spite of her pain, and she is an optimistic person. She graciously allows people to give of themselves to her and her husband, Mark. He is suffering from the effects of long-term cancer. He also knows how to graciously receive service from others. He shares Miriam's philosophy on the merits of receiving and giving. Miriam and Mark, as they are able, frequently offer their own acts of kindness to others. They both radiate light and love because they have a clear understanding that truly, giving is receiving, and receiving is giving.

Chapter 3

Mary, Martha, and the Garden

The intention of this book is to bring awareness to anyone wanting to cultivate a more generous heart. The principle of showing love to others by giving acts of kindness crosses all cultures, peoples, and religions, as evidence of human kindnesses are frequent the world over. The purpose of this chapter is to define the distinction between the types of service that can be rendered. There is a very good story in the Bible that illustrates these kinds of service. It is used as an example because of its simplicity and clarity. It is not offered to promote Christianity.

The setting is in the home of Mary, Martha, and Lazarus. Christ has come to visit. Martha is concerned for the physical comfort of her guests and goes about preparing a meal. While Martha is engaged in this evidently needful activity, Mary places herself at the feet of Christ to be nourished by the spiritual food he offers.

Julie is a woman I admire for making a lifestyle out

of serving other people. She explained part of her service philosophy using this simple story. She stated that there are Mary and Martha types of service that are offered. Martha was concerned with satisfying the physical needs of her guests. Many acts of service require physical attention; needs of food, clothing, or shelter, for example. This is what Julie identifies as "Martha" service.

Mary was concerned with her personal spiritual hunger. Just as there are obvious physical needs to be satisfied, emotional and spiritual needs are also extremely important to nourish. They are not as obvious, so it becomes more difficult to know what is needed. Many people suffer from emotional wounds and scars that cannot be seen. Their cries for help are much harder to detect and are often overlooked. Sometimes people mask their depression or despair or pain so well that no one would have a clue that anything was wrong emotionally. "Mary" kind of service responds to these less obvious calls for assistance.

Each kind of service, whether it is the Mary type (spiritual/emotional comfort) or the Martha type (physical comfort), is equally valuable and useful. One does not supplant the other. They are both viable and complement the full range of an individual's needs. Martha demonstrated her perception of her guests' needs and offered service that satisfied those needs. Mary responded to the emotional and spiritual food Christ was offering. We, too, need to have more perceptiveness to the Mary or Martha kinds of service that are all around us.

Awareness

During many of the interviews I enjoyed with my contributors, the most frequent suggestion I received, besides taking food, is to develop an awareness of others' needs. Awareness is defined as being *mindfully conscious and alert.* Many contributors said something similar to, "Observe the situation, analyze the needs, and then fill the space."

Developing the ability to be attuned to others' needs and assess situations that require assistance is one of the first steps in mastering awareness. Pay attention to the circumstances and settings that surround you each day. Try to pick up the message or meaning of what is not being said. When you ask someone, "How are you?" be mindful of more than the verbal response. Many people will hide their real needs with a well-versed, "I'm fine." So a companion question to this one is, "How are you feeling?" or even better, "How does that make you feel?" It's a question that forces a more in-depth response and may allow you an opportunity to discover more distinct needs, which allows your service to be more effective.

Pay attention to their body language. There may be a particular look in the eyes that conveys worry or upset. Body posture may be giving silent signals of "I need help." Look for rounded, defeated, sagging shoulders. Perhaps you see tension in the jaw, or maybe you just sense that something is not quite right. Responses like these are red flags that indicate there is more going on inside, which betrays the rote answer you will probably get of, "I'm fine." Read behind the eyes and between the lines of vocal expression. I would, however, caution you not to overdo your interpretation or read too much into something. You don't want to be considered a busybody; neither do you want to communicate a message of disinterest. It's a fine line.

Many years ago Katy and her husband had moved to a new city with two small children. One day Katy went for a walk, accompanied by her two-month-old and sixteen-month-old babies, which she pushed in a stroller. After a while she realized she was no longer in familiar territory and had become lost. She walked and pushed, walked and pushed, thinking that surely she would find her way home any minute. Katy was hot, tired, frustrated, and worn out from pushing the stroller. The children were miserable. They, too, were hot, tired, and hungry. Their crying only contributed to her personal stress and frustration. In the middle of this confusion, a couple of women with whom she had become acquainted saw her and stopped their car to say hello. Katy informed them that she was not sure how to find her way home. The women gave her directions on how to return home, said goodbye, and drove away. Considering her circumstances and obvious distress, Katy was more than a little surprised that they did not offer her and her children a ride home.

This is a simple example of not being aware of another's plight. My friend still remembers the incongruity of the situation twenty years later. To effectively comfort someone else, you must sharpen your awareness of the needs and circumstances of the people around you. It is a basic steppingstone in developing your ability to serve others.

The Garden

After Julie explained her philosophy of Mary and Martha types of service, she expanded her thoughts to include a deeper, more intimate, long-term gift from the heart. She compared her philosophy of this kind of service to the experience Christ endured when he was in the Garden of Gethsemane. Before His torturous episode of the night's trial and the agonizing death on the cross the next day, He experienced personal suffering and agony in the garden that no one on earth, before or since, can comprehend. It was intense, solitary, excruciating, and long. In the garden He supplicated his friends to "watch and pray." He sought and needed their support and attentiveness to help Him bear the heavy burden. They did try to stay awake, but each time He petitioned their help, they soon drifted to sleep again. It was a trial of affliction that was His alone to endure.

So it is with people who suffer intense trials and afflictions that can last for days, months, or even years. The adverse conditions can be long, painful, intense, and solitary. Ultimately, it is wholly personal. It is a journey on a path of self-discovery never imagined. It is heartbreaking when all you can do is be there for them, observing the struggle. Yet sometimes that is enough. These long roads of service stretch out in front with what appears to be no end in sight. It can feel disheartening and overwhelming. This is the kind of trial Julie refers to as a personal Garden of Gethsemane.

For sufferer and server, the way is long and arduous and often lonely. At times your offerings of comfort seemingly do little, from an outsider's perspective. Sometimes your intentions are misconstrued. Julie recalled being at the bedside of a dear friend, Sue, who was in her last battle with cancer. Sue and her immediate family requested Julie's assistance but felt it would not be in Sue's best interest to have other people coming and going. Sue and her family felt that she didn't have the stamina and strength to endure the constant activity. The people who did not know of the well-defined request assumed that Julie was deliberately keeping them away. They formed unkind attitudes and opinions of her. For Julie, it was a difficult time knowing others felt unkindly toward her. She persevered in her loving service because she knew her own intentions, the wishes of her dying friend, and the family's desire to protect their loved one from stressful exhaustion. Eventually the neighbors and other friends and acquaintances were made aware of the specificity of the family's desire to keep Sue guardedly cared for during her final days.

This is a poignant example of a Garden trial and service. Much of this kind of living is happening all around us. During these Garden experiences, the sufferer and the giver are being taught divine lessons that are personal and intimate. The lessons are revealed only as the traveler walks the path of experience. They are individually tailored for each person's benefit. So the giver and the receiver are mutually taught and edified. The Garden trial and service can provide invaluable life-changing moments.

Whether the service is an emotional act of listening, a physical act of bringing in a meal, or long-term assistance for a chronic situation, each gift from the heart honors the quiet dignity and majesty of those involved and exemplifies the better nature of humankind.

Chapter 4

A Word about Grieving

When you encounter a person who is grieving, it can be a difficult, uncomfortable, or even embarrassing incident. It is easier to drop off a casserole with a minimum of contact than it is to stay with grieving individuals and allow them to display their grief. Some people find it very awkward when confronted with another's pain. They simply do not know what to do. By understanding the grieving process, we can be more effective in giving loving support to those who grieve.

People grieve for all sorts of reasons. Grief can be due to the loss of a dream or the absence of something important to you. For example, grief could be the result of a relationship one may never experience, such as not having a mate or not knowing a father or mother. Grief can also be caused by the loss of a job, a pet, or a keenly desired promotion. Grief may come from any number of dreams that didn't materialize. Grief can be caused in ways that defy comprehension.

Learning about grieving from your own experiences teaches

you about the composition of grief from inside the feelings. With personal insight and acquaintance with grief, you develop an ability to express a compassion and empathy that can be healing for others as they experience their own losses. Having lived through your own personal grief adds credibility to the love, compassion, and nurturing you gives to others.

In "An Etiquette for Grief" by Crystal Gromer, she elaborates on specific ways we can conduct ourselves. In this article Ms. Gromer states, "I've discovered there is an etiquette for grief. It is not so much a set of rules as a way of being; it requires accepting a place for sadness, for something that cannot be fixed. As a result, it runs counter to cultural assumptions that we must unlearn."

She continues:

> Creating an imaginary worse scenario doesn't make the real and current one better. It trivializes it. The rest of us need to acknowledge the importance of grief and let it be, not try to make it disappear. Often we refrain from saying something meaningful because we're afraid it will hurt. Of course it hurts. But pain is not the worst thing in the world. Embarrassment isn't, either, and that should be the lesson for those who'd like to help. Evasion is worse. Forgetting is worse. The giving and receiving of solace are the most deeply human of activities. An etiquette for grief should help us live with what is hard—and share what is heartfelt. [5]

Grieving has everything to do with reconciling and coping with personal loss. It is the process of trying to reclaim some sense of emotional balance while getting on with life. The amount of time it takes to move through this process is different for everyone. It could be weeks, months, or years. If the grieving individuals know that you respect their personal timetable for grief, it grants them the dignity and freedom to find their emotional equilibrium. Eventually the balance will come, stimulating a desire to engage more fully in life.

The cycle of the grieving process has been well documented by Elizabeth Kubler-Ross. For years she made it her life's work to understand the dying process, the death experience, and the grieving cycle after the loss. She identified the main stages of grief as denial, anger, bargaining, depression, and then acceptance. In her book, *On Grief and Grieving*, Ms. Kubler-Ross goes into great detail regarding each stage of the grieving process.

In "denial" we are merely trying to survive. Once beyond that stage, we enter an "anger" phase, where we begin to function again but new feelings of sadness, panic, hurt, and loneliness appear. As Kubler-Ross points out, anger can be directed at the loved one, the doctors who couldn't save your loved one, or yourself, for being left behind and/or not seeing the crisis coming, being helpless to stop it. We must be able to feel this anger in order for it to dissipate. As we adjust, we enter the "bargaining" phase, allowing us a time to believe we can restore order to chaos.

Next "depression" sets in, which, though heavy and dark, is usually our body's normal way of shutting down so we can adapt. Finally we attain "acceptance," where we learn to live with the new reality, sad as it is, and heal. These stages are not linear; they may come and go, and they may last minutes or months.

Anyone who has ever gone through a death or extreme

loss knows that it feels like your heart is being ripped out of your body. It is like the whole world should stop and acknowledge your pain. It is a wave of disbelief that washes over you when you realize the world continues to function on every level while you feel like you are drowning in sorrow. These are the moments of poignant grieving. They are solitary experiences. There is no help for it but to face the grief, express the grief, move through the grief, and then somewhere along the path, let the grief rest.

A friend of mine who experienced the loss of her husband at any early age described her experience with grief.

"How does it feel? It is a very real physical pain. It is like nothing you have ever felt before. You can be doing anything: driving, sitting at home, watching TV, and all of a sudden this wave of grief comes over you, and you dissolve in tears. One of my friends said she thought if she turned around she would see a trail of blood behind her, her pain was so great. This is normal. There is no shortcut, and there is not a set amount of time allotted to accomplish it."

Perhaps with a better understanding of grief and the grieving process, those of us who want to alleviate a little suffering of others can do so with more compassion. Remember, grief is a powerful, overwhelming sadness that catapults people to explore and experience other emotional offshoots that may be a surprise for them. Grief visits people for many reasons, whether it is a loss of a variety of life situations, or it is the ultimate loss caused through a death. I offer a gentle reminder that it is important to become acquainted with the grieving process because we will all grieve at some point in our lives.

Chapter 5

The Heart of Listening

Are you aware that the word listen contains the same letters as the word silent? During my research, "just listen" came up more often than any other suggestion. It is the simplest form of kindness one could offer and seemingly the most needed. However, I think silent listening is more difficult than it might indicate. It is a common human tendency that as we listen to someone telling us about a painful experience or the details of their current emotional upheaval, our minds are actually very busy doing just the opposite. While we pretend to be listening, what we are really doing is choreographing a pithy reply, sage advice (most likely unwanted), or even ruder, a comparative story of our own. So be careful to not give into the temptation of wanting to fix their problems with your advice or suggestions. More often than not people just want to know that someone is really listening to them.

With that in mind, then, as you interact with people

going through difficulties, let them talk about whatever they feel a need to express. As you visit with them, remember, you are there to listen. You don't need to do anything else. Often what is most soothing and satisfying to the one in need is to have a trusted sounding board. Reassure them you are there to listen to them. You might offer openings such as, "Are there any feelings you would like to discuss? Are there circumstances that you want to explore? Do you want to talk about whatever comes to mind?" Whatever they divulge, a simple, soft reply of validation is usually helpful.

Initially it may be uncomfortable for you to allow people to grieve openly with you, to allow them to shed tears and express their anguish. When these deeply-felt emotions and intimate feelings are shared, don't be afraid of the tears. Remember that crying is cleansing and promotes healing for the griever. If you listen with your heart, let your compassion show in your eyes. Hold your friend's hand or briefly touch her shoulder with tenderness. You don't have to do anything, really. Just listen! But listen attentively. Here is a list of particularly important guidelines:

- Allow them to finish their thoughts and sentences completely without interruption.
- Keep "war stories" of similar experiences to yourself.
- Stay in a non-judgmental place.
- Unless you are asked for your opinion, refrain from giving advice.
- Keep these personal conversations private.

When you practice these guidelines, the grieving person's

confidence in your concern for her increases significantly. She must know she is safe in your hands. This is important in her healing process. If she senses a compromise in your ability to fully listen, stay interested, or if she learns that you repeated to others what is personal and private to her, it only adds to her pain while revealing your lack of character.

Emily Post's common-sense approach to listening appropriately is good counsel. "Empty other thoughts from your mind and concentrate on what the person is saying. Then show that you're not only listening but understanding by making eye contact, nodding occasionally, and intermittently saying, 'I see.' If you don't understand something, ask for an explanation, a habit that comes naturally to a good listener."[6]

Remember that an effective "I see" reflects an interest in the person who is talking. Being fidgety or restless, losing eye contact, and interrupting are all dead giveaways that you simply are not that engaged in the person's thoughts or feelings. It would be better never to have offered a listening ear if you can't be truly present for this person. As one woman expressed it, "Having a listening ear doesn't require supplying an answer."

The heart of listening is learning to hear the quiet voices that speak to your soul in the stillness. I'm referring to communication patterns of the soul to which every person has access. There are a couple of "voices" that I would like to highlight. They are soft and nonintrusive but instructive. Being aware of these patterns is the first step in going beyond a physical awareness of someone's needs. Becoming familiar with them and then activating these patterns of communication allows you to be more effective, especially when the needs are not obvious.

The Intuition of Your Inner Voice

Each of us is born to this life with an inner navigational guidance tool. It is called the inner voice. This inner voice is the expression mechanism of our pure and higher self. It is a personal well of wisdom. If we cultivate the physical and spiritual environment of our lives to reflect enough quiet, peace, harmony, and order, this allows opportunities to fine-tune our receptivity to the voice of our inner selves.

It's important that we make room in our day for quiet contemplation, meditation, and prayer. Here's an idea. When you are compiling your list of things to do for the day, write down a specific time of day when you can slow down and turn inward. As you refer to your list throughout the day, you will be reminded that this quiet time is a part of the day you have planned and is as important as taking the kids to their extra-curricular activities or the run after work. This daily practice contributes to an environment of stillness and helps discipline the mind to let go of its mental chaos. In this way we align our sensitivity to the communication frequency that is given to us in soft, gentle ways. As wisdom unfolds and we give attention to that wisdom, we become more familiar with these whisperings. With sharpened "inner ears" we can use the wisdom, insights, or information we receive to benefit other people's lives, at the same time refining the quality of our own lives.

At times we are uncertain and doubt the information we hear from this inner voice. In the book *The Dynamic*

Laws of Prosperity, Catherine Ponder suggests, "Perhaps you have not followed your intuitive leads because they have seemed fantastic, and you have waited to reason through its promptings before you chose to act. Intuition is not concerned with reason, for intuition…does not explain. It simply points the way, leaving you free to take it or leave it, to heed or ignore its promptings."[7]

Part of your responsibility then is to trust the intuition, respond to the information, even if it doesn't make sense to you. The more you apply yourself in the service to others based on this intuitive lead, the more comfortable you will become with this process. It will yield wonderful experiences for you.

Promptings or Nudges

Promptings are impressions you receive from a spiritual realm outside of yourself that quietly guide and cue you. They are given as energetic nudges, instructions, or directions, which give us valuable information. Often these promptings propel us to do exactly the right action for the good of another person. These impressions can be as subtle as a feeling or a fleeting thought. For example, you may be randomly thinking of someone and in that moment receive a phone call from that exact person or get information about that person that leads you to helpful action. These promptings can also be as dramatic as a clear voice in your head and as audible as talking with a friend face to face. When you pay attention to the promptings and impressions you get and then act on them, you will always benefit from the results of your actions.

I have learned to heed these promptings and impressions with more confidence. I listen more attentively to my intuition. It is a distinctly subtle but powerful signal. When I pay attention and follow the guidance I am given, it always serves my best interest. The many contributors of this book have also become astute listeners to their impressions. They are familiar with how their souls hear this communication. Because of practiced trust in their promptings, many kind deeds result from paying attention to these voices of the soul.

Let me illustrate with a simple example. A woman purchased a plant for herself and distinctly felt that she should buy two plants. She knew she didn't want two plants but purchased the extra one anyway. Later, when she had some quiet moments, she asked for guidance through prayer regarding who needed the second plant. A name dropped into her mind. She took the plant to the woman named. The woman was surprised by the visit but was grateful for this act of love and attention she was not expecting. She had a need that was unknown by the giver of the plant. But because attention was paid to an impression, both women were blessed, and a heavy heart was lightened, which resulted in a tender exchange of love and gratitude.

Small acts of kindness, such as the one noted above, are generally the most frequent, because they are the most needed. Dramatic incidents usually capture the headlines. But the quiet and simplistic acts of love that produce no public attention are generated from carefully listening with spiritual ears and then following through with some kind of action that is consistent with the impression or thought. These acts have the power to change people's moments, days, or even their lives.

Silence

We live in a very noisy world. Television, movies, cars, planes, radio, iPods, cell phones and crowds of people are all constant sources of background noise to which we have become accustomed. For example, if there is silence in the car, a common reaction is to turn on the radio or put in a CD. Many people simply do not like silence. I know people who will turn on the television just to have noise in the background because they are not comfortable with silence. However, if one allows silence into one's daily routine more often, it can serve to be a conduit of information to help others.

Silence is a valuable tool to use in centering yourself. Make use of this quiet time to reject anything that could be distracting your attention. It takes discipline to get the mind to quiet, but it is so effective in helping to keep the noise chaos at bay. Stay focused in the present moment. There is magic in the silence. You will amplify your listening skills tremendously. There is enchantment in your inner voice and in your promptings. You will come to enjoy your own quiet company.

To become an effective listener, you must seek silence in your world. This promotes stillness inside of you. The stillness is the receptive center for hearing your impressions. Use stillness and quiet to your advantage. For example, if you are in conversation with someone who is expressing personal and intimate information, there may be moments when lulls in the conversation occur. When these pauses come, listen for any promptings or impressions you are being given. You may receive specific guidance on how to help this grieving individual in front of you. Trust these impressions implicitly. Act on them quickly for the greatest effect and benefit.

Never underestimate your intuition. It is tempting to second-guess your instincts or what you sense. Be careful of being dismissive of your impressions. Learn to trust this soft inner voice that is gently guiding your life. It has been given to each of us for personal guidance and as a source of direction to help others. Trust the impression, take action, and follow through. Once you make this a familiar pattern of living, your spiritual ears will pick up many directives that are regularly given to you. You will be amazed at how useful this resource is in guiding your daily path. Be alive to your promptings and the wonderful ramifications that will flow from that awareness. Intuition, your inner voice, promptings, silence, and stillness create the heart of listening!

> "We need to find God, and he cannot be found in noise and restlessness. God is the friend of silence. See how nature—trees, flowers, grass—grows in silence; see the stars, the moon and the sun, how they move in silence...We need silence to be able to touch souls. In the silence of the heart God speaks. Let God fill us, then only we speak. Do small things with great love. The fruit of silence...is prayer. The fruit of prayer...is faith. The fruit of faith...is love. The fruit of love...is service."
>
> —Mother Teresa[8]

Chapter 6

Creative Ideas of a General Kind(ness)

You see the problem, you listen to your inner voice, and you know who needs help. Now what? At times it's hard to know just what to do. The next two chapters are written to give you ideas you can implement. Many of the ideas didn't fall neatly into one particular category. For general acts of kindness, the following suggestions are mentioned in this chapter to use as your own judgment and discretion dictate. A few of the suggestions, such as using notes, cards, or letters, could easily be used for any of the specific categories outlined in chapter seven. Because of its universal necessity, food would also be useful under most circumstances. Some ideas may not ever feel comfortable for you to use. I would encourage you to use your imagination to tailor any of the following ideas to express your own personality. Draw from your life experiences to enhance your personal touch. Enjoy the growth, the journey, and have a rewarding adventure!

Use a Friendly Approach

If you have the desire to lift a stranger's day and leave him with a feeling that he matters, you can accomplish this with a sense of play, modest humor, and/or exuding a kind and loving energy. Each of us can help ease the tensions of the day. In doing so, we are serving another human being. It costs nothing. However, it does require moving your ego and self-consciousness out of the way. You will be surprised at how many people respond as if they are experiencing a breath of fresh air. Try it!

A good friend of mine loves not having any hair. He has had no hair for years. His line is, "Bald is beautiful." One day he and his wife were waiting to catch a flight home, and he spotted a younger Asian man sitting alone, sporting an extreme Mohawk hairstyle. He promptly walked up to the young man, sat next to him, and forthrightly asked him, "Why did you cut your hair like that?" His question was not asked in judgment but curiosity. He loves being bald. He simply cannot understand why a man would want to waste time with having hair, let alone styling it, especially in a very attention-getting way. This question opened a conversation with the young man that lasted through their mutual flight to Salt Lake City. The young man remarked to my friend just before deplaning that the flight they shared was the most enjoyable flight he had experienced in a long time. Because of an impulsive act to cheer a stranger, my friend and this young man developed a friendship that continues to this day.

Because my friend has practiced, polished, honed, and used a friendly approach for so many years, as he gently engages strangers to feel uplifted by him, he never comes across as threatening, judgmental, or abrasive. In fact, he has a look about him that invites people to engage in conversation with him. He told me it is a self-imposed, everyday assignment to seek out someone whom he feels could use a little cheer. At times he does encounter suspicion and reluctance from people who simply refuse to have their spirits raised, particularly from someone they do not know. But he persists, and it does not take too long before he can at least get them to smile.

I have seen his infectious delight with life and his youthful exuberance when he succeeds in drawing people out from behind their emotional walls of protection. I admire his ability to interact with people in this way. These brief interactions continue to feed his own well of personal joy, in addition to spreading joy and happiness to others as he travels throughout his day. If we have the courage, we, too, can learn this simple lesson of using a friendly approach with strangers as we circulate through our tightly-packed days.

Listed below are wonderful ideas that will give you a place to start. As you effectively make use of any one of these suggestions, you will contribute positive, loving energy into the lives of those you serve, as well as continue to replenish and fill your own well of joy. This list is a beginning. There are many ideas not listed that you could add as you become aware of them. Keep the inventory of ideas and suggestions growing.

Let's talk food!

Food probably tops the list because it is such a basic necessity. It is human nature to want to give comfort and love with food. Taking the time to prepare and bring food to dispirited people seems the most obvious and natural act of kindness. This will always be appreciated since stressful situations are usually times when families or individuals least want to be bothered with cooking. So we offer food. It is part of our make-up to want to take care of the physical needs of those we care about. Remember Martha? Here are a few pointers when offering food for comfort and need:

- Try to keep the food healthy. Treats are fine, but giving only sugary items is not beneficial for any kind of healing, whether it is physical or emotional. Give sugary foods sparingly.

- Snack trays are a good idea. Finger foods are also great. These offer smaller portions for those who find eating a whole meal difficult.

- Be sensitive to the dietary requirements and needs that your intended recipient may have. For example, it is important to know ahead of time if there are dietary restrictions or guidelines that need to be followed, such as those for diabetes, food allergies, medication compatibility, heart conditions, high blood pressure, and so forth. If you get specific information about a person's food restrictions, share it with those other individuals who are also contributing food items. The offerings are always meant well but are ineffective if they cannot be consumed.

- Try not to offer anything that is too rich, too gourmet, or simply too awful. Make sure that homemade food is a tested recipe that has been well received by others. If you do create something from your kitchen, use recipes you know are sure winners. If you offer purchased meals, be aware of the sugar and salt content. It may be too much for those receiving the food. Try to buy or make healthy, tasty items.

- Organize and delegate a group of volunteers who would be willing to provide nourishment for a family or an individual if the need is over an extended period of time. This helps to alleviate a cost issue and gives more individuals the opportunity to serve. At the outset of this service, be clear about how often the food is needed so that the volunteers are ready to provide meals for as long as necessary.

- Be sensitive to cultural tastes. What is common and liked by one culture is completely unfamiliar in another. It is wise to have an understanding of what the family or individual enjoys and can tolerate. If there is misunderstanding, the time, effort, and money that are put into the food may be wasted.

- Deliver meals in disposable containers. There are many different plastic, microwaveable containers that are on the market today that make these offerings a no-brainer cleanup. Also, it eliminates the need for the recipients to be burdened with remembering to return the dishes or bowls.

- Have ingredients on hand for a quick and easy recipe to whip up if you find that a meal needs to be taken in to someone.

- Use a recipe that could easily be doubled and freeze the extra portion for an emergency situation.

- Similarly, freeze the leftovers to keep on hand in case someone outside of your family needs the food on a moment's notice.

- Helpful hint: make minibread. If you don't have a minibread pan, bake the dough on a cookie sheet in the shape of French bread.

- Let your children help deliver a meal or a treat to someone needing help or even just a little cheer.

- Send out for pizza and have it delivered to a family as a surprise.

- Invite some friends over for lunch, just because.

- Making a family's dinner is a nice relief for the family cook if you know that he/she has an especially busy week.

- Share the produce out of your garden with those around you.

- Pick up some extra produce during the summer harvest, when produce is on sale, and share with friends, neighbors, or acquaintances. Perhaps you could include an uplifting note with your gift.

A Message about Notes

This was another frequently suggested idea. Notes are easy, personal, quick, creative, soothing, and can be read over and over again. My daughter has written numerous notes to me that are thoughtful, love-filled, and tender since the day she could pen two words together. She has given me dozens of notes over the years, for all kinds of reasons. They are some of my favorite treasures.

Notes may be written to someone just because you are thinking about them. Leave them on the windshield of a car, on a pillow, porch, or any other creative place you know your intended recipient will find it.

A friend of mine keeps every note and thank you card she receives in a special box. When she needs an emotional boost, she will re-read the cards, and it lifts her spirits tremendously. After she shared this with me, I gathered my notes and cards and have them stored in my own special box. I can truthfully say they have sustained me during some low points in my life. You may want to give it a try.

When occasions arise that are of a more serious nature, notes need to be specific to the situation at hand. Notes ought to be filled with words of love, encouragement, and appreciation. When a person is having a rough time, she may value a great quote or an uplifting thought that is pertinent to her situation. Remember to say something positive about the individual receiving the note. Perhaps she has a talent or a character trait you appreciate, or she conducts herself in a way that is admirable. Mentioning anything positive and specific about her will boost her mood, and she will know that someone took the time to give her attention. It might be just the tonic she needs to get through the rest of the day.

E-mails are considered notes, not as personal as hand-written expressions, but great for extremely busy schedules. They also come in handy when you have an impulsive thought and want to connect with someone quickly. If you have to look for writing materials, the information may be gone in the time you spent looking. The spur-of-the-moment action of e-mailing saves embarrassing moments of memory lapse. It is my best communication venue when I want to act on an impromptu impulse.

Keep inexpensive cards or notes on hand. Get a year's worth of thank-you cards, birthday cards, "thinking of you" cards, etc. (See the list below.) Remember to have a supply of stamps also. Carry a few cards with you in your car, your purse, or your briefcase. Make a master list of addresses of family, friends, business associates, your church congregation, or other contacts. Many of us get impressions to "act now." If we are equipped with simple materials, we can follow through on the impression and not lose an opportunity to lift someone's spirit with a note of remembrance. Send notes for the following occasions:

Birthday	New job
Job well done	Congratulations
Encouragement	Anniversary
Thinking of you	Graduation
Sympathy	New baby
Friendship	Get well soon
New move	Retirement
	Bon voyage

General ideas for all sorts of occasions

- First and foremost, be willing.

- Be prepared to offer help. If you can, leave a little room in your day so that you have flexibility and time available at a moment's notice.

- Give a homemade or store-bought blanket or smaller quilt that is soft to the touch. Blankets or quilts are often comforting and help to promote relaxation.

- Find out what the individual likes to read and check out books on tape from your local library that would suit this person's interest. Re-supply as the need and desire continues.

- Give a fluffy and soft toy animal. It's like a blanket. People love to hug something close to them when they hurt.

- Offer to cut the lawn, pull weeds, plant flowers, or help with other yard work.

- Find out what a person likes and what their individual interests are. Put together a basket or small, clear plastic gift bag and fill it with items that would be heartwarming. (Gum, a chocolate bar, a pen, a personal note, an uplifting quote, a small book, bubble bath, or candles are all good ideas.)

- Make a telephone call that communicates, "I'm thinking of you."

- Present a journal to someone dealing with an affliction or other difficulties. Encourage the person to write about the experience. This could be beneficial at the time and perhaps more so when their hardship is over. It is cathartic to express true feelings and thoughts on paper.

- Ask pointed questions. For example: "Do you need me to drive you to an appointment? Do you want company? What kind of food is appropriate to bring to you? What about your housework? May I vacuum for you? What is your most pressing need at the moment?" Any such questions that get below the surface response of "I'm fine" are what you need answered. The answers will provide the necessary information to help you more accurately assess the needs.

- Pray! Never underestimate the power of prayer! You may receive the name of someone that you had no idea needed any help or attention. Also, you may get a very specific idea of service to do.

- Show up and listen. See chapter five.

- Have baby gifts on hand. Watch the sales and have that pink and/or blue gift available to be able to grab and go.

- Keep tissue paper and gift bags on hand for the times you want to do something spontaneous for someone who might need a lift.

- Give a call to someone you think might be struggling or just needs to vent.

- Give a potted plant with the necessary instructions for its care.

- Buy a live plant and offer to plant it in their yard.

- Prepare bouquets of flowers, if you have a cut-flower garden. Take them to anyone you feel needs a lift.

- Remember that a smile and a hello can be the easiest and most frequent act of service that you can offer.

- Join a weight-loss group with that friend who wants to lose "those last ten or twenty pounds."

- Offer service in an area of your expertise, such as counseling, law, finance, accounting, hair cutting, or music lessons. Depending on the situation, you could trade services. It helps to make people feel less dependent or in debt.

- Offer to assist in outdoor yard work as dictated by the season and region you live. For example, shovel snow for someone and maintain such caring service as necessary.

- Always look ahead at your week and know what you have on your calendar. If something develops that needs immediate attention, you will know the degree of flexibility your schedule allows. Being aware, you can readjust your schedule as needed. It helps avoid the "I'll get back to you" approach. In other words, plan to be spontaneous.

- Clean the headstones of the local cemetery. This service is especially effective during those times of year when attention is given to the people who have died, such as Memorial Day and Veterans Day.

- If you have a talent that would be helpful or useful to others, offer that service. For example, if you sew, and you know someone who needs help with mending clothing or costumes, offer this help.

One friend of mine told me the following story: "I was on the costume committee for Annie Warbucks. Becky was in charge of all the costumes, and she hadn't asked me to do too much. About two weeks before the play opened, I figured she must be swamped, so I asked if there was anything more that I could do. She said she had it under control—she just needed to make ten more maids' aprons. I pressed her and finally got her to let me make them. I know she would have gotten them done, but I am sure she had other things to do for the play (in addition to taking care of six kids!). I like to think I was able to ease her workload a bit. Maybe she had time to do something fun with her kids that she wouldn't have otherwise."

- Solicit a teenager whom you know to deliver your anonymous gifts.

- If you notice a woman struggling with kids and groceries in the store parking lot, offer to hold the shopping cart and/or load the groceries into the car for her. This allows her to give her full attention to the children's needs and get them securely into the car.

- Offer to carpool to school, sports activities, dance lessons, etc., for the family in crisis or need.

- Offer to be a chauffer for someone who does not or cannot drive. Some situations might include doctor appointments, grocery shopping, or running errands.

- Create a care package for the family members and/or siblings of those individuals who are recovering from a crisis.

- Offer to help clean and maintain some level of organization in the home during a recuperation period.

- Tie a group of colorful balloons to someone's door or mailbox to give that person a lift.

- Encourage the person going through a rough period to write about the experience. It is healing to express true feelings and thoughts on paper.

- If you are housebound or elderly but capable of limited service, consider making regular calls of encouragement to people in difficult situations who need a friendly voice. You could also make birthday greeting calls to your friends, family, former business associates, or church acquaintances.

- Consider allowing a family in need of temporary housing to stay with you if circumstances are appropriate.

- If you are an elderly or mature person, pay attention to the younger generation. Compliment or nurture them, as you feel comfortable. Generational friendships provide perspective about the other generation that generally one wouldn't be aware of. They also help people move out of predictable patterns of interaction with their own age group and promote personal growth in ways not imagined.

- Share money. Give it anonymously in a card with a note of love and encouragement to a needy family or service-project fund. Have the children in your family contribute to the fund. This will encourage their natural generosity, as well as help the children feel they are important members of the service project.

- Prepare a talent show. Use your family's talents, as well as children in the neighborhood or other interested people who want to share their talent. Present it to senior centers, homebound individuals, or anyone who would enjoy this kind of cheering up.

- Organize a neighborhood party once a year. Close off the street if it is approved, or hold it in a park. Have a couple of getting-to-know-you games.

- Introduce yourself to a new neighbor and make the newcomers feel welcome. Express positive statements about the neighbors, the community, and the activities that are available. Be respectful of their desire for privacy if you sense they don't respond to the enthusiastic welcome to the neighborhood.

- Volunteer to teach English to those who don't speak English if you have language skills. What a great service to offer to others!

- Help people from other cultures get the resources they need, for themselves or for their families, that are offered by the community.

- Compliment someone on a talent you know he has, or when he shares the talent, praise him for his efforts.

- Look for ways to bring a smile to a retail clerk who is helping you. This is easy enough to do with a sincere compliment, an easy joke, or an uplifting conversation. Treat him or her with respect.

- Volunteer to help someone who has a home business during the times of the year that are particularly busy. For example, a woman who had a home business knitting hats was especially busy during certain times of the year as she prepared for fairs. A couple of friends volunteered to price her items and help her organize the product so that she could concentrate on finishing production.

- Offer to assist with water-heater or soft-water-systems repair if you know of elderly, widowed, chronically ill, divorced, or single individuals who may need it.

- Never forget the chocolate, except when dietary needs dictate otherwise!

Chapter 7

Do Something! Specific Ideas for Specific Situations

This chapter is the heart and soul of the book. It is filled with recommendations that have proven successful in easing burdens. There are twenty-seven categories of needs, crises, or situations that are common to the human experience.

Because a variety of people contributed the suggestions, the ideas are as diverse as the people who offered them, giving you a lot of choices. You will find ideas that fit your timeframe, pocketbook, talents, and comfort level. Take the core concept of the suggestion and adapt it to your personality. Be flexible, because a lot of times other people's needs come at an inconvenient time for us. Be realistic as well. Sometimes we are in a position to offer more of our time and means than at other times. Do what you can, but most of all enjoy the opportunity to help one, one, one.

A Word of Caution

In your enthusiasm to offer help, be sure you do so with the intention of following through. When you ask the question, "How can I help you?" be prepared for the answer. It may require something as small as washing someone's breakfast dishes and straightening the living room, or it could develop into service that will require weeks of attention. Barbara's story will help illustrate my point.

She had answered a phone call from a neighbor to assist in processing the newly arrived evacuees from Texas who had lost everything in the devastation of hurricane Katrina. Barbara's willingness to help her neighbor fill this need required her and her husband to sacrifice the time they set aside on Saturday for mowing the lawn, catching up on laundry, and doing their weekly shopping. As she moved among the shocked and numb survivors, she approached a woman named Kathy and asked, "How can I help you?" Barbara was unprepared for the answer.

Kathy responded, "I can't find my children." Barbara knew in that moment her involvement was going to be much more than assembling boxed lunches and handing out clean T-shirts.

Barbara began her journey with telephone calls to Kathy's extended family in North Carolina. She spent hours and hours on the phone piecing together a way for Kathy to find her kids. She worked with organizations such as the Red Cross, the Salvation Army, and CBS. After several busy days and sleepless nights, the reunion was successful—but Barbara's volunteerism didn't end there.

Because of the trust she developed with many of the evacuees, Barbara continued to assist them by finding willing, local people to aid them as they began to rebuild their lives within their new communities. Several weeks after answering a call to help and asking the simple question, "How can I help you?" Barbara was still involved in helping the evacuees make smooth transitions into a new environment.

Based on Barbara's example of selfless love and willingness to ease the way of strangers, I became aware that one must have complete honesty in heart and sincere intention to follow through to the end—no matter what is required. When you ask the question, "How can I help?" be prepared for whatever the answer. Go the distance even if it requires much more than you imagined when you offered to help.

The suggestions that are listed are not designed to be all-inclusive. Obviously, there are endless possibilities, especially when you put your own personality in them. As you learn to magnify your abilities to help others, add your own ideas to the lists.

Abuse

The definition of abuse is "to treat in a harmful, injurious, or offensive way, to speak insultingly, harshly, and unjustly to or about." Abuse in all its ugly forms is unfortunately prevalent in our society today. The personal humiliation and shame victims feel from the abuse is seldom broadcast. Many victims choose to protect and excuse their perpetrator's actions. Until the victims are ready to face the truth and take action to protect themselves against these evil violations, there is not much others can do except encourage them to get help and support.

In the meantime, if you are aware of abuse going on with someone with whom you have a trusting relationship, consider some of the following suggestions. One or more of them may help alleviate suffering. She may feel, with your support, that she does have a place to start to get out of the destructive pattern that has become her reality.

- Help her get professional counseling.

- Listen to her story without judgment and advice. See chapter five.

- Remind her with the following:

- Believe in yourself!

- You are a strong woman, even if you feel inadequately weak at the moment.

- You are not a loser but a normal person caught in a dangerous relationship.

- You can rescue yourself.

- Offer her a list of helpful books and/or other resources if you feel it would not be considered intrusive.

- Go with her to a support meeting. Support meetings are very helpful because the participants can perceive that, like her, other women are also caught in unhealthy relationships. Such meetings can strengthen her resolve to make the necessary changes and will help her rebuild self-esteem.

- Encourage him to extend himself to others in the group and serve them as he is able. This can happen once he has established trusting relationships with the other people in the group. Focus on his talents that would be beneficial to some of the other people in the group.

- Inform yourself regarding abusive relationships. Such knowledge will provide you with a deeper understanding of the cycle of abuse and may give you insight into specific ways to help in specific abusive situations.

- Insert yourself into her life lovingly but assertively, as a friend, by offering your help at whatever level is needed.

As an example of this, I recall attending a weekly meeting for abused women to listen to a well-respected woman recount her story of abuse and her victory over the situation. She had holed herself away from society for about a year because she was so traumatized and depressed from her experiences of abuse. Finally, one day a neighbor who had become a friend literally pulled her out of bed and forced her to help clean her own house. She insisted the abused woman stay busy and get back to living her life instead of hiding in the mountains. She was consistent in maintaining her friendship and offering help. Another friend offered to tend this woman's children once a week so that she could begin her college education. This second friend offered her service for a year. Eventually this victim of abuse earned her doctorate, found a great job, and was able to take care of herself and raise her children.

Encourage the abused person to extend herself by helping others. As she lifts the spirits of other people, she will
lift her own spirits. By doing so, she can awaken an understanding of her own value as a woman. It could give her the
strength to stop her personal cycle of abuse.

Many of the ideas in chapter 6 are worthwhile in offering support and love to an abuse victim.

Bring her a delicious chocolate treat and together watch a
humorous girl movie! (When the timing and mood feels right.)

Accidents

Accidents are just that—unplanned and unexpected disrup-
tions in the flow of life. They are inconvenient and extremely
frustrating. Some accidents are as minor as an irritation, and
others are huge hiccups. Sometimes people return to the life
they knew before the incident. However, some people experience a complete change in the landscape of their days for the
rest of their lives. Whatever the case, accidents are common
occurrences in all of our lives. The specifics of the situation,
of course, will determine what kind of help to offer. The ideas
in chapter 6 may also apply to many accident situations.

If there is a serious accident:

- Offer to help transport family or relatives to the
  hospital.

- Offer to make phone calls to notify family or friends
  of the accident.

- Make sure that neighbors know about the situation (without being a busybody). This may help to

develop a support group for the family. Immediate or sporadic attention may be needed while recuperation is underway, and proximity may be an important consideration.

- Check with the family to assess any help you may be able to offer regarding physical necessities from home that they will need during a hospital stay.

- Attend to the house if the family is going to be away for a while. Light housekeeping and any obvious yard work would be helpful. Maintaining the appearance that the house is occupied is important.

- When it is appropriate to visit, take magazines, books, books on tape, and CDs of soothing music. See the section on hospitalization for other ideas.

- Offer emotional support. Make a phone call to encourage the accident victim and/or the family. Stay in touch every few days. Even a short, "I'm thinking of you," call is meaningful.

- If the victim is a young adult, encourage other young adults to take interest in the person, thus helping with the recuperative process.

A young adult friend of mine broke his jaw a couple of years ago. Consequently, he had his jaw wired shut for three months and was unable to eat or drink. He was able to get nourishment by letting liquids seep through his teeth. A friend of the family brought over several milk "chugs" in a variety of flavors. The note attached to the gift said, "We heard about your broken jaw. Keep your chin up."

This simple gesture of remembering a friend's trial was very meaningful to Josh. Even though his mom and even the woman giving the gift couldn't remember the details of the gift two years later, Josh remembered in detail. It had an impact in his life during a time of great suffering.

- One individual learned from her own experience that it is important to not judge the person who is injured. She had felt impatience and frustration from family and friends because her healing process wasn't as quick as they were told by the medical team, nor was it as fast as they had expected. They intimated by their comments to her that there was something she wasn't doing that impeded the healing process. Remember, everyone heals at his or her own progressive rate, physically and emotionally. Don't assume the accident victim should heal at the rate of your expectation.

- If the family would appreciate a helpful call to their spiritual leader for support, let them know you can make this call for them.

- When the person is feeling up to interaction with you, take him a favorite chocolate treat and a great movie!

Addictions

"It takes a big heart to help an addict."

—Julie

Both the addict and those who love the addict suffer. Because the world we live in is infused with people who have addictions of all kinds, there is so much suffering that occurs, and millions of people are affected by addiction behaviors and consequences. Sometime in our life there is a high probability one of the following situations will develop: we will become aware of one or more people we know who are addicts; we will be affected personally by an addict's behavior whether we know them or not; or we will have complicated relationships with an addict. Whichever the case, we need to increase our understanding of addiction and codependency. If we become more knowledgeable about addiction behaviors and recognize the signs of addiction, we may be more effective in minimizing the disruption and damage done in an addict's life, as well as in the lives of the addict's loved ones.

There are many useful and informative resources on the Internet that address this topic of addiction. I use the following information from a site called Visions. "Addiction is a dependence on a behavior or substance that a person is powerless to stop. Addiction has been extended to include mood-altering behaviors or activities. Some researchers speak of two types of addictions: substance addictions (for example, alcoholism, drug abuse, and smoking) and process addictions (for example, gambling, spending, shopping, eating, and sexual activity). There is a growing recognition that many addicts are addicted to more than one substance or process."9 The following two quotes gives us more insight on addiction and the common occurrence of a behavioral interaction family and friends develop with the addict called codependency.

Codependency is a term often used for the spouses, children, or other family members of the addict. When people become codependent, they begin to focus their lives solely around the addict. They make decisions based on if the addict will affect any possible situation positively or negatively. They begin changing their own behaviors based on the addict's behaviors or wishes.

Families, friends, and employers of addicted people often don't understand an addict's seemingly chaotic mindset. They witness the addict behaving in perfectly normal ways, arriving at work on time, paying bills, and spending time with their family, and then the next day or even the next hour the addict becomes immersed in the depth of their addiction again. When addicted people feel the need to feed their addiction, they think of nothing else. Their one thought, their one urge is to indulge their craving. It is during these times that the addict is in their most irrational and uncaring mindset. When the urge to indulge their addiction has taken control they are concerned only with satisfying that enslavement; absolutely nothing else matters. They will miss work, abandon their family, and neglect their own health in their pursuit of a fix. The future simply does not matter and they do not consider the negative consequences that will come about as a result of their single-minded focus.[10]

The following suggestions are directed toward aiding and sustaining the addict's support system (i.e., family, friends) and the addict through difficult times:

- Encourage the individual in his recovery process. Offer emotional support. Let him know he has what it takes to stay whatever course he chooses.

- Do not judge nor criticize those who love the addict. These people need positive feedback. Love them and reassure them that they are wonderful people.

- Send a card with the message, "I'm thinking of you."

- Stay in touch with positive, uplifting conversations in frequent phone calls.

- Lend a listening ear. See chapter 5.

- Don't try to fix it for him. Sometimes the spouse of an addict hasn't figured a way out of the relationship, or if he chooses to stay, he needs to figure out how to live with his reality. He needs to have someone to talk to about his situation. Many times these support people glimpse the true and wonderful nature of the addict, and they cling to the fantasy and expectation that one day the addict will live life from that part of herself on a regular basis. That hope is what keeps the support people involved with the addict, even though they know intellectually that it is a harmful relationship.

- Refrain from asking questions such as, "Why don't you tell her 'this' or 'that'?" or "Why do you put up with her behavior?"

- When visiting with parents of a person dealing with drug addiction, mention the good qualities and characteristics of their son or daughter. The parents need to know that the addiction is not all that people see in their child.

- Offer any healthy act of love and service that you think would be appropriate. It sends the message, "I'm thinking of you." This is sometimes all that is needed to give an addict the courage to face another day. See chapter six.

- As you are able, encourage the support system of family or friends to learn how to serve the addict effectively.

- One woman who was in this situation suggested it is very important to know how to balance your life. Coping with an addict is very consuming, both in time and in the emotional arena. If you don't pay attention to your own needs, you can easily become resentful and empty of feelings of love or wanting to help. You have no energy to give anything to anyone, and you lose the ability or desire to grow personally.

- Help your friend to focus on balancing her life by encouraging her to engage in activities that she enjoys doing. Give her opportunities to do what she wants or needs to do.

- Pay for and book, a manicure, or pedicure for her.

- Offer to pay for and book a massage! (Make sure she doesn't mind being touched by a stranger.)

- Reassure this person that he or she is not crazy! A very important suggestion I received from several women.

- Invite this person to healthy social gatherings that you know she would like.

- Encourage family and friends to learn about the addiction.

- Establish and maintain firm boundaries. Do not equivocate. Do not vacillate. The tough love method is important to maintain with this approach.

- Do not rescue her! It is very tempting to want to help by relaxing the boundaries when you see her having extremely difficult times during the recovery process. It is uncomfortable to observe as she attempts to remain strong, go through withdrawals, or struggle with extreme emotions. If you rescue the addict, you are doing great harm to her and only trying to assuage your desire to make the road to recovery easier for her. The progress she is making has then been compromised. You are now pegged as someone she can take advantage of when she wants to manipulate a stressful recovery situation to her benefit. She now has the upper hand. Codependency rears its head in these situations.

- Attend twelve-step programs with the addict. It will give you a real insider's point of view and also educate you in specific ways that will help you encourage the addict to stay strong and focused on her recovery. *The twelve steps are:*

  1. Admit powerlessness over the addiction.

2. Believe that a power greater than oneself could restore sanity.

3. Make a decision to turn your will and your life over to the care of God, as you understand him.

4. Make a searching and fearless moral inventory of self.

5. Admit to God, oneself, and another human being the exact nature of your wrongs.

6. Let God remove all these defects from your character.

7. Humbly ask God to remove shortcomings.

8. Make a list of all the people harmed by your wrongs and become willing to make amends with all of them.

9. Make direct amends with such people, if possible.

10. Continue to take personal inventory and promptly admit any future wrongdoings.

11. Seek God through meditation and prayer.

12. Carry the message of spiritual awakening to others and practice these principles in all your affairs.[11]

• Help the person locate and use the community resources that are available (i.c., counseling, lawyers, support groups, etc.).

• Do not judge the person.

• One woman noticed while she was in the hospital that the medical staff was very generous in doling out pain medication. It was very helpful when she needed it, but after a while she felt mentally fuzzy and physically not in control. She reduced the amount taken and felt more pain but less dependent. She cautions overuse of prescription drugs.

• Enjoy a delicious chocolate treat together and a humorous movie!

Being Single

I had not even considered this category until one of my girlfriends pointed out to me that many single people get swept to the sidelines of life. They may have willingly chosen to remain single or have not had the opportunity to choose a partner. Either way, being single is a tough status for some people, and they can get lost in our family-dominated society if we are not careful to include them.

Obviously, there are always those individuals who love this lifestyle choice and thrive within it. They can usually assuage their loneliness and aloneness with confidence and capability. They have figured out what fills them up or satisfies their emptiness. However, every now and then, they need a loving nudge from someone, sometime, to get them out of their "singleness" thinking and enlarge their scope by helping others and letting others help them.

My girlfriend has a loving and wonderful sister who has never married. They both received great learning experiences when her sister lived with her and her family for several years. Shay enjoyed the caring, loving attention and help Kappy gave her children. The children observed another terrific female role model as they developed an intimate lifelong love and friendship for their aunt, and Kappy learned about the dynamics of these relationships while being part of a young family. Although this living situation was extremely difficult and stressful for everyone, it was ultimately a complete win-win. There were many occasions when personal interests were sacrificed for the good of the whole family unit. Everyone learned important, and sometimes painful, lessons of the importance of living a more selfless life.

Of course, not all single people will have a similar positive experience, nor would some want to even entertain this kind of arrangement. But it is an option. Here are some suggestions to consider when you have an opportunity to serve a person who is single:

- Probably the easiest and most effective thing to do is give them a phone call with a message of "I'm thinking of you" and expressing genuine interest in their day-to-day activities.

- If distance is an issue, drop a note in the mail every now and again. Give suggestions for a great read, a new recipe to try, or a movie you enjoyed and would recommend.

- Invite them to family gatherings as much as is comfortable. Seasonal celebrations are very important to maintain traditions and memories for some people.

- Set up a tradition in your life with this person to have them to dinner on a weekly or monthly basis.

- Invite a single person you know well to prepare a dinner for your family every now and then. Suggest a "country of the month" idea. Have everyone in the family contribute to the meal.

- Let the person demonstrate or even teach you or your family about a special skill or an interest at which they excel.

- If this single individual is musically inclined, invite them to share their musical talent with your family and/or friends on occasion, such as holding "musical evenings."

- If there is a certain level of trust and a known history of the single person, let that special person contribute to the lives of your children in an inclusive way, such as reading with the children, tending the children when you go on a date with your partner, helping with school assignments, and being invited to share in some of your family and/or holiday activities.

- Invite/include this person in your community, faith, or civic activities as well as book clubs, hobby classes, and other such group happenings.

- If there is interest shown, introduce this person to your circle of friends.

- Suggest they participate with you in charitable work in the community.

- See chapter six for ideas that would be appropriate for someone in this category.

- And of course, enjoy time together with a chocolate treat and a fun, humorous movie. If chocolate isn't their flavor of choice, bring them a treat you know they like.

Chronic Illness

This is a difficult category, simply because chronic means long lasting, persistent, and recurring. Cancer, neuropathy, bipolar conditions, AIDS, burns, heart problems, and obesity are just a few of a long list of chronic illnesses that plague people. The support systems for these people can become strained over a long period of time, and the loved ones simply get worn out. It is very needful to offer appropriate assistance when there are long months and sometimes years of maintenance and/or recovery. The family and/or caretakers of the victims/patients welcome temporary relief from their responsibilities of caretaking.

A friend of mine has cancer. He has a remarkably positive spirit and exudes an upbeat optimism. He and his wife have undertaken a very daunting and serious battle to overcome this disease. When his news became public, one of their friends was simply unable to verbalize to him face to face her feelings of sadness that he had to deal with this harsh reality. She wanted very much to let him know of her support and love. One day my friends found a package on their doorstep filled with "Mr. Incredible" trinkets and gadgets. It was her way of conveying to them her feelings of sorrow for their trial and her love and support for them during a difficult time.

Here are some more suggestions:

- Sometimes with long-term care, the recipient needs to establish a trusting relationship with the person who offers his service over a period of time. This could be seen as a testing period. The receiver may suggest small needs at first to determine if, in fact, the one serving will follow through. It is disappointing to depend on a person for promised help, only to realize it is not going to happen.

- Treat the person with respect and dignity. Don't act as if the person is dying or at death's door. This is one reason some people may not want to volunteer information about their health situation. They want to be treated as they have always been.

- Send notes or cards on a regular basis with uplifting, inspirational, and positive thoughts.

- Offer to sit with the person, if needed, during difficult times of the day or night. This also helps relieve the long-term caregiver.

- Regularly run errands for the person and/or the family if they are unable to get out of the house. For example, pick up groceries, go to the pharmacy, take them to doctor appointments, or purchase small household items.

- Repair and maintain the home as needed. If the job

is too big for you, enlist the necessary help—after receiving permission from your patient that it is okay.

- Stay in touch on a regular basis with cheery and uplifting phone calls. Refrain from asking, "So, how are you today?" with every conversation.

- Offer to take care of their pet or pets on a regular basis if your time and distance allow.

Chronic illness can also be a major financial strain. A great service, apart from giving money, can be organizing fundraising events. Following are some ideas:

- When children in a young cancer patient's neighborhood would hold birthday parties, they would ask for donations to his cancer fund instead of accepting presents for themselves.

- Sponsor a lemonade stand for children and give the raised funds to the ailing person.

- Have a bake sale and donate the funds to the family of the chronically ill person.

- Sell bandanas. Consider imprinting a personalized message on the bandana that inspires people.

- Rubber bracelets with a personalized message or reminder are one way to keep attention focused on the ill person's chronic situation. These could be sold with the person's name engraved. Donate the funds to the family or to the person with the illness.

- Enter a sponsored marathon or walkathon.

- This is time and case sensitive: take a chocolate treat of their choice, and include an uplifting, humorous movie!

Death of a Loved One

There is nothing in life that prepares a person for the permanent departure of a loved one. It is unnatural to our sense of continuity and the familiar. Even when the loss follows months of declining health and you know intellectually that a person is going to die, when the moment of death occurs, it is a surreal experience. There seems to be no way of preparing emotionally for the loss. Perhaps nothing is more heartbreaking than losing a member of one's family or someone extremely close to your heart. Shock sets in immediately, and it is difficult for the mind to grasp the reality of what is evident—that your loved one is not coming home.

When death becomes a part of your life experience, important lessons can be learned. There is the lesson of coping with loss, the lesson of discovering the depth of your own emotional strength, the lesson regarding your own mortality, and the lesson of understanding compassion, to name a few.

If you have not yet experienced this particular personal loss, the suggestions that are listed will help you feel a little more comfortable when you desire to comfort the mourner. It is important to remember to visit the family when you are feeling strong, especially if you, too, have been emotionally affected by the passing of their loved one. It is unfair to go and offer your condolences, and then when you are overcome with emotion, receive consolation from the family! It is worthy to mourn with those who mourn; however, you do not want to end up burdening the family with your grief.

Everyone has a personal way of handling grief. Some people want to keep busy and avoid home where memories are most tender. Some individuals want only to stay home and for a period of time avoid interaction with others. Others may not want to be left alone at all.

For example, two women in the same neighborhood lost their husbands within months of each other. Both families include several children. One woman did not want to be without her kids. She found strength in their companionship and their energy. She needed them around her. The other woman found it soothed her emotional state to have some time away from the children. She needed the quiet time to help center herself, and the physical rest allowed her mind to settle and her body to regain strength.

In whatever situation you encounter, remember to be sensitive to the needs of that individual or family. One person's needs may be exactly the opposite of someone else's needs, as in the above example. Ask specific but sensible questions that will help you get clear answers. For example, "May I take your children overnight?" If the answer is that she would rather keep her children close, offer to lighten some physical burden. Keep an eye on those who are grieving and respond according to their needs.

Don't be afraid to call. Don't hide. This applies even if you do not know the individual or family who has just lost a loved one. Sometimes friends or acquaintances disappear following a tragedy because the impression is that they believe their friend or friends need time to grieve. They don't need to be abandoned! Observe respectfully from a slight distance but always with the intention of being there for them at a moment's notice. Check in with them to assess the needs, and if the time to help still isn't right, that's okay. Stay close and observant and respond when you feel the time is appropriate.

My cousin Karen was relating an experience she had of assisting an elderly woman in the last days before she died. Initially, with some reservation and questions, she agreed to help this woman. For several months she gave physical, emotional, and spiritual comfort as the woman continued to decline. My cousin was at her bedside with the woman's family when she died.

Karen gets emotional telling this story because, as she served, she learned to love this woman unconditionally. She also realized what an honor it was for her to share in this very sacred experience called death. She says, "Everyone wants to be present at the beginning of someone's life—why not the end?" My point here is to encourage us not to be afraid of the anticipated death. Offer love, a generous heart, and gentle service to the one who is transitioning from this life. The lessons will continue to flow. It is a gift that the dying person leaves with you. Even if your efforts feel inadequate, do something!

- Call and check regarding the convenience of stopping by to give comfort to the family.

- Offer to make phone calls, if appropriate, to inform friends or distant relatives or out-of-town family.

- Stop by to give a hug. Perhaps simple condolences are appropriate for the moment. When the moment is right, just listen to their grief or comments. See chapter five.

- One woman showed up with a mop and cleaning supplies. She invited the widow to go to her bedroom for some quiet rest or reading or relaxation while she cleaned her house.

- Taking this idea one step further, organize help to have the house cleaned, dinner delivered, and the children occupied with friends. This service would allow the parent to have needed time to him or herself.

- A recently widowed acquaintance suggested the above idea was wonderful; however, for her it was important to also have an activity preplanned. She felt that having alone time was too painful, and she needed an activity that would distract her. She appreciated the efforts of her friends when they would create space for her to be by herself and would also give suggestions or plan something for her to do during that time away from the demands of home and family.

- Often the family doesn't want to leave their home. The traffic, noise, and crowds can feel overwhelming. Offer to run some errands for them.

- Be sensitive to visiting too long. These longer visits should probably wait until after the funeral. The family is usually exhausted and emotionally spent, so keep visiting brief.

- Refrain from lecturing, trying to comfort with stories that "are worse than this," or staying too long. Acknowledge the person's and/or family's pain and let them talk, cry, or vent their anger. A hug, simple words of comfort, and expressions of love and support are appropriate. It all helps.

- Get help or do some of the yard maintenance. A clean and neat yard is easy on the eyes when the family comes home from errands. This isn't something people are inclined to take care of when death is lingering.

- After time has passed, don't forget your suffering friends. Give them a call, especially on the anniversary of the death of their loved one.

- Keep a calendar of events that have transpired so that you can remember to stay in touch at the appropriate and meaningful time of year.

- When time has elapsed after the death, food offerings may continue to pour in. Remember to keep the food healthy and nutritious. No one needs extra sugar or sweets available all the time. One woman said she felt the thoughtfulness was generous, but she and her children didn't need the extra calories. She found it difficult to turn down generosity, because she didn't want to hurt feelings. She preferred healthier food if it was going to be given to her family.

- Along that same line, if the main provider of the home died, consider giving the family money instead of providing meals. The meals are thoughtful, but the family, knowing their own intimate needs, can use the money in specific ways that alleviate some financial strain. (This is a great way to help the family after the shock has lessened and life begins to resume a somewhat normal pace.)

- Instead of bringing in meals, buy gift certificates for local restaurants, grocery stores, or other local stores you feel would help the family or individual.

- Poetry is helpful and sensitive. Buy a book of poetry that is edifying and comforting; present it wrapped in a simple, but lovely way.

- Send letters, cards, or notes with uplifting themes. Keep the message positive.

- Get babysitters for the children, and keep them occupied. Sometimes they get neglected or are in the way. This can help distract their attention from the tragedy.

- Bring healthy breakfast food. This is seldom remembered.

- Bring light snacks and grazing foods. These are good items to have on hand, as sometimes a big or heavy meal is not what the family has the appetite to eat.

- If applicable, help the person find something on which to focus his or her mind to keep it active and functioning. This is helpful, as the mind is unable to stay focused for very long during periods of grieving and loss.

- Put anonymous flowers at the gravesite whenever you think about it.

- Allow mourners to confide anything, and remember to keep your tongue quiet.

- Wait a week or two and then check back with the family. Take a meal in when others are no longer offering help.

- Flowers are always welcome. Make sure there are no allergy-sensitive people.

- Green plants in pots will be a lasting memory after the blooms fade from bouquets. Make sure there are instructions as to how and when to water and how to tend to the plant.

- Keep sympathy cards on hand. They aren't the cards that we normally would have handy but are very good to have ready to send as soon as you hear of the loss of a loved one. Often people don't know what to say or are worried they may something inappropriate. I found the following statements are warm and meaningful without being too familiar or common. "I am sorry for your loss. My heart goes out to you and your loved ones during this very difficult time." "Please know that you and your loved ones are thought of with gentleness and concern during this difficult time." If you are not comfortable with a personalized message, sign the card with warmth in your signature, such as, "With loving thought," "With warm affection," "With fondness," etc.

• Write a letter to the grieving family about the loved one's influence in your life. Give specific examples.

• At a viewing I attended, there were 3 x 5 cards available for the mourners to write their feelings down about the deceased. This was done while they were waiting to pay their respects. After the viewing the cards were gathered and given to the family. They felt comfort and appreciation knowing how many peoples' lives their loved one had touched.

• On the day of the viewing, offer to take in a meal before or after. The family is always exhausted and may not take the time to eat. Note: bring food that is nourishing. A platter of cut-up fruit and vegetables is great. Several kinds of small finger-sandwiches are wonderful. Refrain from heavy foods or too much sugar. The family's stomachs are already churning, and this kind of food is a poor choice at this time.

• After the passing of a loved one, help clean and organize the home. If it is an elderly relative, select special treasures and share the stories. Help pack and then clear away boxes and leave the area tidy.

- If death and the funeral occur out of town, cleaning the home of the one who is experiencing the loss can be very helpful. Sad and unexpected news such as this creates the need to drop everything and depart for the destination. It is so appreciated to come back to a house that is clean and organized.

- If you have scrapbooking or video skills, put together a photo album or video with pictures, meaningful songs, etc., along with letters and stories as a memory for the family and a tribute to the one who has died.

- Make a CD of music that is soothing and meaningful to help the grieving process.

- Keep phone calls infrequent and short.

- Refrain from asking personal or detailed questions regarding the circumstances surrounding the death. If the family member wants to share these intimacies, they will do so on their own volition.

- If the death occurs in the home and smaller children are involved, suggest that you take these children to your home for a while as the family gets details planned.

- Purchase a bleeding heart plant and plant it in the yard of the family with their permission. When you feel it appropriate, share with the family personal experiences of the deceased loved one, or send a note or letter of condolence if you did not know the deceased.

- Make a pillow out of some of the deceased's favorite clothing.

- Have a pleasant and appropriately positive attitude. Grieving is exhausting. However, try not to be exuberantly cheerful.

- After the funeral, stay in touch with the family. Do not overdo your attention, however. Drop in a meal once a week. Make a quick phone call. Offer to go for a walk with one of the family members. Talk about things other than just the recent death and current situation. Most people don't want to feel like the local charity case. One gentleman got sick of people always asking, "How are you doing?" even months after his wife died. He just wanted to be treated normally again. Be sensitive about knowing when to stop inquiring after their emotional state.

- Offer to help fold clothes and clean out personal effects of the person who died. This is difficult for family members to do, as the wound is raw, and they have a hard time because they recollect their loved one in the clothes and using the personal items. If the clothing is not to be distributed among the family, perhaps take them to a shelter for people who could use the items.

It took several months before one of my girlfriends could even think about moving or changing anything that was her husband's clothes or personal items. She needed the comfort of seeing the items in exactly the same place they were when her husband last used them. It can be a sensitive subject, so offer your help gently and carefully. If the family is not ready to take this task on, keep in touch and then gage when it might be appropriate to offer your help again.

- During Thanksgiving dinner, one family member began the meal with remembrance of the departed loved ones and mentioned his gratitude and love for all those at the table because of life's uncertainty not guaranteeing that all of those present would be at next year's dinner.

- Verbalize your memories of the departed one.

- Share experiences with the family or individual of how you have handled the death of a loved one. Do this after the funeral when there is not so much for them to think about. Be sensitive to its usefulness.

- When appropriate, and if you know them well, include them in service that you are doing for someone else.

- If you are a close and trusted friend, sort through the mail. Eliminate the junk mail and simplify and organize the remainder into orderly piles of bills, correspondence, magazines, and so forth.

Speaking to someone who has suffered a great loss can be uncomfortable and awkward, especially if you haven't experienced a personal loss yourself. In most cases, be sincere and go with what your heart tells you. Still, some statements are better left unsaid. The following are examples of insensitive comments that were told to me as being offered as condolences. In my opinion, they are simply inappropriate and potentially hurtful.

"Well, at least…" These statements are meant to console, but they leave the broken-hearted individuals with a feeling of hollow condolences.

"He or she is better off now. He or she suffered so much."

"Now you can get on with your life."

"Boy, you sure have a lot of lonely years ahead of you."

On the other hand, several phrases or comments can uplift, inspire, and soothe. Try some of the following appropriate things to say:

"I'm sorry for your loss."

"May I bring you dinner tomorrow night?"

"She was such a wonderful person."

"He was a great example to us all."

"I would love to help with your services. May I greet your guests or make phone calls for you?" and so on.

Depression

In my opinion, depression is more widespread than most of us realize. Sometimes it is obvious to recognize; more often than not it is a subtle emotional state that goes undiagnosed or ignored. Depression is a common response to many of the crises that are addressed in this book. It can be a temporary condition lasting a few hours, or it can manifest as a chronic condition lasting years. Whether depression is triggered by outside events or is the result of a chemical imbalance, it is important to know how to render help and assistance to the sufferer. It is not necessary to know what caused or contributed to the depression, but it would be very helpful to those who want to render assistance. Knowing the root of the cause would give one a clearer picture of the sufferer's situation and contribute to useful ways to help alleviate the depression.

One woman said she kept returning to a friend she knew was at home and was experiencing a deep depression. She would knock and knock again, with no answer, then leave a simple gift at the door. She told me it took about seven times to knock and leave a gift before the friend had the courage and energy to open the door and invite her to come in. Her friend apologized for being so evasive, and expressed her appreciation for her friend's persistence in coming again and again to leave a gift of love and thoughtfulness. Eventually she was persuaded to get involved in some charity work herself with her gift of needlework. This service was a beginning step in counteracting the depression she felt. It helped pull her out of the darkness she was experiencing.

Sometimes it does take persistence to make a difference in a depressed person's life. By offering ongoing, loving, nonjudgmental gestures from the heart, such persistence may bring a measure of needed relief. The depression may not be completely lifted, but your consistency does let the person know you care. It may contribute in assisting them develop a strength and determination that contributes to their ability to move out of the darkness. Your efforts do matter. Here are some ideas:

- If a parent is depressed and needing outside support, explain the situation to the children at their level of understanding (regarding the parent suffering from depression, assuming you have a relationship with the family and have their approval).

- Involve the children with your children in healthy and meaningful activities such as outside sports activities, simple community service, or music lessons, if appropriate.

- Keep the children busy. Give them responsibilities around the house to alleviate the parent's load.

- Offer to drive the depressed person to doctor appointments.

- Send the person notes with positive quotes, funny sayings, or encouraging words. Make this a weekly occurrence as long as you feel it is appropriate and is something to look forward to as the tradition develops.

- Take your friend to see someone who is also in need of a visit—perhaps a homebound individual or someone who is recovering from surgery. The list of reasons is endless. Loving service usually lifts the person who lifts another!

- Be persistent. The depressed person may not want any visits. You may get rejections to your offers of help, using a myriad of reasons. Keep going back.

Reassure the person of your love. Be gentle in your voice and sincere in your offerings. Eventually you will gain a level of trust from the person. She needs to know you are honest in your desire to help.

- Try to discover a talent or gift this person has that could be useful to others. They may be willing to share it with others who are in need.

- Offer or arrange for occasionally needed assistance with housekeeping for a person in which a chemical imbalance causes sporadic mood changes.

- Encourage those on prescription drugs to be consistent with their medication.

- Tape a church or spiritual meeting for the "shut-in" and present the tape that same day.

- One woman had witnessed her friend go through a particularly difficult year with surgeries and recovery. She purchased a toy sailboat and gave it to her friend on her birthday with the note, "This is a symbol to remind you that 200_ will be a smooth sailing year."

- Many ideas listed in chapter six are very applicable in this category.

- Share a delicious chocolate treat and a humorous movie with this friend. The light and fun energy of the movie can help relieve some heaviness of spirit, and of course, chocolate is always soothing!

Divorce

Who among us has not been affected by divorce? It surrounds us. We all know someone who has experienced it. Perhaps even you, the reader, have walked down this pain-filled path. If you have, you will appreciate the stress, agony, and grief that are inherent to this dramatic shift in people's lives. It is a devastating and heartbreaking experience to go through, which shatters the foundations of the family unit. The repercussions of the breakup of the family reach extended family members as well. The result is a wake of heartbreak for many people that takes a long time to repair.

With this major life change, the process of separation, reestablishing new living arrangements, and the consequential emotional adjustment are extremely difficult and upsetting. The people involved experience feelings and emotions such as confusion, anger, frustration, betrayal, loss, insecurity, guilt, anxiety, panic, sorrow, and regret. The life that was known and familiar is gone. In its place is an awkward stage of fragmentation and pain that somehow tries to fit in with the activities in life, which continue. Adapting to this new reality is uncomfortable and painful for everyone in the family.

There are many valuable resources available that offer information that sheds light on all the different dynamics of divorce. It's a good idea to have a basic understanding of the stages in divorce that the individuals and family go through. It is important in your own growth for effective service. Your awareness of the acute needs will expand. You cannot know exactly what the individual is feeling, but a fundamental familiarity with the relevant aspects of divorce contributes to the credibility of your intentions to help.

The following suggestions are offered as a neutral place to stay in these uncomfortable times. The proposed ideas are appropriate for both males and females moving through this emotionally exhausting and painful experience.

- Establish a connection with these people immediately. Love them and reassure them. Be aware of their sense of embarrassment and their feeling of a loss of self- worth.

- Stay out of it! Don't allow yourself to get caught in the middle of their conflict or be persuaded to take sides.

- Do not judge either party!

- Do not change the way you treat either party. Continue to be caring and polite. Wave, chat, make eye contact, or drop a note of encouragement in the mail.

- Volunteer to watch their children, when appropriate, such as when the parent has a meeting in the home that brings up divorce details. In such a situation, it is advisable to have the children out of listening range. Such meetings could include private meetings with counselors, lawyers, or clergy.

- There may be times when the custodial parent needs alone time, without the responsibility of children. Be proactive in helping the parent find a good, trusted babysitter if the parent does not have one. Try to find a sitter that comes highly recommended with appropriate skills and experience.

- Offer to put the children to bed and do the whole bedtime routine! This is assuming you have that kind of relationship. The parent will welcome the respite to be able to do whatever she or he wants!

- If she has a need to talk about her story, be ready to listen to it. Let her talk but remember to not allow yourself to be pulled into a place of choosing sides. If you feel she is trying to sway you to support her side of the divorce issues, remind her that you are there to listen and be her friend and are not willing to get involved beyond that point. Refer to chapter five.

- Offer to take this person to lunch, a movie, or a quiet place for a visit. Just get them out of their routine for a break!

- Ask the individual if he or she is the primary caretaker of the children involved and what his or her needs are regarding household functions. Such needs may include limited childcare, house cleaning, meals brought in. Offer what you can if it is appropriate.

- Encourage your friend or friends not to make rash decisions that will affect them long-term, such as immediately selling the house, changing the children's schools, or quitting work.

- Suggest they find a positive support group if you feel it is appropriate. Consider going to the first several meetings with them to ease the way into a strange environment. Although it may be initially intimidating, the benefits of a support group are great.

I feel the following quote from Divorcemagazine.com is instructive in broadening one's awareness in regard to just how much emotional support people going through divorce need.

"Eventually, even the best friend will burn out, though: long before you're ready to stop talking about your divorce, your friends will have tired of hearing about it.

"The benefits of joining a support group—or going for individual therapy if you're not ready for the group experience—cannot be overstated. A good support group is not 'a bunch of whiners' or a forum for male or female bashing. Rather, this is a collection of people at various stages of the divorce-recovery process who can offer advice, assistance, and the reassurance that your negative thoughts and feelings are completely normal—and that they will pass. Members of a divorce-support group have stood in your shoes and can demonstrate by example that a better future is just around the corner for those willing to take the steps to get there."[12]

- Encourage them to rekindle interest in previous passions they had, such as ceramics, dance lessons, hang gliding, hiking, martial arts, painting, or papermaking. The list is obviously person-specific. Try to draw from them their interests and help them get started again.

- Offer to do some house cleaning or laundry while the parent uses this opportunity to take the children to the park, the movies, or any other activity they haven't had time to do together as a family.

- Bring supportive, encouraging articles or books on the healing process and the road to recovery from the divorce.

- Do something fun with them, and avoid talking about their current situation. They need a healthy, fun time away from the emotional trauma.

- If both individuals happen to be your friends, reassure each of them that in spite of the current, pending divorce, you still value their individual friendships.

- Bring your friend a chocolate treat and enjoy an evening with her while you watch one of her favorite movies.

Elderly

Many of today's elderly have lived from the first automobile days to man living on a space station. They have experienced life from agriculture being the major economic contributor of America's stability and success up through the technological stampede and takeover of the information age. Staying current with all these diverse changes and adjustments in their lives speaks to their adaptability, which cultivates self-reliance and a sense of independence. These elderly individuals have proven they are capable and competent in staying equal to or ahead of the times.

For many mature individuals, years of making decisions, dictating the direction of their lives, rearing children, and experiencing full and responsible careers have all added to this sense of capability. At some point, however, one of life's frustrating ironies rears its head. The irony is this: wisdom increases, and the lessons that life has taught become understood, an acquired patience for the rhythm of life becomes evident, and the desire for physical engagement in life continues. However, the body begins its decline and gradually loses ability and strength. I have heard it said that the "golden years are laced with lead." How frustrating and upsetting it must be to realize the abilities and activities that were once so effortless are now an exercise of struggle and disappointment, as well as trying to get used to strange aches and pains that never existed before. One would wish we could have the body of a healthy twenty-five-year-old without losing the wisdom acquired with age!

These dear mature individuals may not have pretty, trim, and youthful-looking bodies, but in many ways they still feel young inside and want to relate to younger generations. Perhaps they don't see as well, or perhaps they have difficulty hearing. Maybe they talk more slowly than is comfortable for you to listen. Generally, they will walk more slowly than you do. Whatever the physical impairment, remember never to be dismissive of them! They would love to be able to have full function of their bodies. After years of self-reliance and independence, it is difficult to feel comfortable accepting help from others. Most elderly people do not want to ask for help even when they know they need it. Be polite, patient, and courteous to them. Show them respect and be solicitous to them, because they are your elders.

Assessing and reassessing elders' needs is important. Understanding their abilities to manage their own needs is important. If you underestimate their abilities, the inclination then is to overdo, making it easier for them. This is not necessarily in their best interests. It takes away the opportunity for them to retain a needed degree of independence. Reassessing their needs and abilities is important as well, especially while they are moving through a period of recovery and/or rehabilitation. For example, if the individual is sick and unable to drive, arrange for this service as needed. When the elderly person gets better but is still in a weakened condition, it might be in his best interest to encourage and teach him how to take a bus, if appropriate. Developing new skills and abilities preserves a person's dignity during this transitory period.

Remember that each individual is an incredible person! You may not agree with their reasoning or philosophies. You may even dislike some of their firmly held opinions regarding politics, religion, or any number of attitudes and beliefs gleaned over a lifetime; nevertheless, each elderly person is someone worthy of assistance. Serve them now as you would like to be served when you grow old. Below are some examples of giving service to the elderly:

- Offer your time to listen to their history. Ask about their family, their friends, and their work experiences.

- Record their history on tape. Ask them questions about:

- Their ancestry.

- Current information and stories about themselves, their spouse, and their children.

- Memorable work experiences.

- How they handled some of life's common challenges.

- Lessons they have learned about living.

- Vacuum their cars or home. (Bending and maneuvering such equipment may be difficult for them.)

- Assist with appropriate outdoor chores, such as shoveling snow, tidying the garden area, and taking out/in garbage and/or recycling bins.

- Offer to drive them to their appointments, or do necessary and/or fun shopping with them.

- Offer to clean their floors, dust their furniture, etc., depending, of course, on their living arrangements.

- If they are in assisted-living or nursing home situations, decorate their rooms as the seasons change.

- Offer to give them a ride to one of their favorite places, such as a park, the zoo, the beach, the mountains, or an ornamental garden.

- Invite them to your house for an hour or so to give them the opportunity to be around the energy of childhood. They may enjoy reading to your children, or maybe they would prefer to be an observer. If they have no family close, they need other company, and mothers, now elderly, miss the energy and excitement of children.

- Invite them to go to the park with you and your children so that they can delight in observing children at play. Pack an extra sandwich and have them bring one of their food specialties if they would like to do so.

- Shop for their groceries if needed. Make it an occasion the elderly can count on.

- Respect and acknowledge them with simple, consistent attention, whether it's a hello or a regular phone call.

- Bring live music into their homes. Hold a small musical event that won't weary them, but will give them a boost, while sharing your musical talent and/or that of your family.

- Assess their talents. If they have talents that could be used in the community, encourage them and set up a network for sharing their gifts. If they have products that could be sold, encourage them to continue to produce them, while you find a source to sell them.

- Help with their funeral plans if appropriate. Carry out the plans as they have desired, if it is appropriate for you to be that involved.

- Celebrate their birthdays with them. You could have a simple cake and card party or more elaborate plans with invited guests.

- Assess their diets. Often they lose interest in eating properly. Make sure they have access to quality, balanced, and healthy foods. Also, bring in help to cook for them as needed.

- Help them to organize their important papers so that they are readily accessible when needed. One such important paper is a one-page medical reference sheet containing all medications, allergic reactions, and a brief summary of medical history with dates, primary doctors, other contracts, and insurance information. This information, along with a copy of a living will and medical treatment plan, should be kept together and quickly accessible in case of a medical emergency.

- Make sure they have a current blood-pressure record when health problems are a constant reality.

- If diabetes is a factor, know where their daily records of blood sugar and insulin amounts are kept. Be capable of drawing the proper insulin dosage and administering the shot. Be sure to have their written permission and consent and their doctor's approval, if needed. If you are not certain about how to do this procedure, make sure you know someone who does who can be readily available if the elderly individual cannot administer this need himself.

- Keep a record of their appointments handy on a calendar.

- Keep such information as family members' names, birthdays, addresses, and phone numbers together in an easily accessible place. This will assist them in making contacts, sending birthday cards, and sending letters or other communications as desired or needed.

- Maintain regular care of the elderly person's computer (if the elderly person has and is able to use one), with timely internal cleanup of the hard drive so that it is reliable.

- Arrange and have family members rotate weeks of visits with activities, talent programs, show and tell, or reading to them to help maintain their spirits.

- Consider devices that can be installed to mitigate the difficulty with some of the physical activities that the elderly may be experiencing. For example, if the elderly are capable of living on their own but have difficulty with strength, balance, navigating stairs, and any other such up-and-down situations, consider installing handles or bars of some kind in areas such as bathrooms, garage areas, stairs, and any other place in the house that would be helpful. Also consider such helps as a seat within a shower stall with a showerhead that adjusts for sitting,

- Bring them a treat and watch one of their favorite movies with them!

Empty Nest

Don't get me wrong. As a parent, you have known and wanted the end result to be exactly this—an empty nest. Your job has been to raise your children to be strong, civic-minded, courteous, kind, independent, and capable individuals who know how to tackle life on their own. As the first chick moves through the teenage years and gets nearer to the edge of the nest, the anticipation of that first flight generally creates considerable excitement for the young man or woman. It can have the same effect on the parents with a good dose of anxiety and hope for good things to come mixed in.

For years we have gathered our chicks under our wings and fluffed our feathers in satisfaction, knowing that everyone is under our protection and care within that nest. Then the day comes when the first chick actually takes flight. What is worse, the next chick is standing on the edge of the nest flapping its wings, testing the air currents, and developing strength for its own flight of freedom. The pattern continues until all the chicks are gone. The nest is empty! There is no more fluffing your feathers, knowing you are protecting them anymore. I felt like I had actually been stripped of my feathers, standing naked and bare and insecure. It was awful. The strange, transitional stage of looking around the nest, knowing the chicks were gone, was very hard on me.

A girlfriend of mine had just the opposite experience. It was a complete surprise to her! She thought she would have that hole-in-the-heart experience that I felt. She did not, to her delight! When her children were on their own, she realized that she was not worrying about them in the same way as before. She knew they were in colleges that they enjoyed. She felt they were grappling with their lives in mature and wonderful ways. She was no longer involved in their day-to-day, hour-by-hour activities and therefore did not find herself consumed with, "Are they going to be home at the appointed hour?" or "When they get home, how many friends are coming with them?" She experienced a sense of freedom that she had not known in years, and a mental burden had been lifted. The energy and mood of the home settled down. This contributed to calming down her soul. It was a wonderfully surprising gift.

Not everyone who experiences the empty nest syndrome gets that gift. Some parents have a real struggle with the whole reality of not having young energy flying in the door at any time, disrupting the home with all the hustle and bustle, and flying back out on a whim! It may be too quiet for them. These parents may find your attention very gratifying. A little support and encouragement from friends, loved ones, and neighbors who have empty nests of their own is a wonderful boon. The following thoughtful acts help begin the process of mending the hole. For those parents who love the new freedom, enjoy your time with new and old friends in a million wonderful ways!

- Present a gift basket or bag with a box of tissues (for dad) and a large, chocolate candy bar (for mom).

- Create a small nest using a colorful bucket with straw or other material resembling a bird's nest. Fill the bucket with fun, personally appropriate gift items.

- Take the parent(s) out for lunch or dinner and ask questions about their now grown-up children. Be interested in their activities. Let the parents talk.

- Encourage the parent(s) to develop personal interests that have lain dormant for years.

- Suggest to the parent(s) that they consider serving a humanitarian mission of some kind, if funds, health, and time allow.

- Suggest community service if it would better suit their time and talents.

- Suggest going back to college as an option if the parents have not finished their education and an interest remains, or even if a new educational interest would sound fulfilling to them.

- Encourage them to volunteer at local schools, hospitals, shelters, etc.

- Suggest sharing of a parent's knowledge, specialty, talent, or a service that he or she would enjoy doing. Such a service might be on a voluntary basis or taught in a school or community at a reduced rate of recompense.

- Invite these people to share an impromptu outing with you. The break in their routine is refreshing.

- Hold a monthly "empty nesters" get-together.

- Suggest they adopt another child when none of the above suggestions helps. (Just kidding!)

Funeral

This is a tough day for the family. Be sensitive about the timing of your visits. The family may not have the energy or inclination to interact with those outside of immediate family and close friends. Preparing for the funeral is a considerable effort, which needs focused attention, and it perpetuates the emotionally draining experiences that come with the recent loss. (A word to the family whose loved one died—*allow people to help*!) The following suggestions will guide you to know what is appropriate service for this tender, sacred, and painful time.

- If you are at a loss as to what to do, call the person in charge and offer your help for whatever is needed.

- Offer to greet the family and friends who come to the funeral home and to direct them, if needed.

- Volunteer to stay in their home during the viewing and funeral. (There are people who take advantage of the family's absence during the funeral service and will rob the home.)

For funeral services held out of town, consider the following ideas:

- Put together an age-appropriate travel kit for the children. Paper, pencils, granola, color crayons, fast-food gift certificates, tissues, raisins, etc.

- Offer to bring age-appropriate books on tape.

- Offer to collect the mail, water their lawn, change lights, take the garbage in and out, park your car in their driveway, or get the newspaper.

- Wash the family's car so that it is clean if it is needed during this time. Also, it is especially considerate to fill it up with gasoline.

- Offer to get the children's shoes and clothes ready for the funeral service.

- Send the family a box of thank-you cards and postage stamps to help them with their responses. Funeral homes usually do not give them enough.

- Donate enough paper or plastic products, such as dishes, utensils, and napkins to last a week or so for the stream of visitors that they may have following the funeral.

- Prepare for freezer storage any surplus food items that have been brought to the home. These foods may be very helpful at a later time.

- Do not stop being a friend after the intensity dies down. Stay in contact with the family and keep offering your love and support.

- Lovingly and tactfully contact the family if you notice significantly changed behavior in your mourning friend weeks or months after the event. If you are close enough to the family, and they have not been physically near enough to notice such changes, tell them of your concerns in case professional counseling may be needed.

- Help set up the meal for the family members after the funeral services.

- At the family meal following the funeral services, arrange the donated flowers and plants in an attractive manner.

- Give financial donations to the family.

- Take the flowers, plants, and other mementos of remembrance that were used at the funeral service to the family home when the service is completed (and make sure they're watered).

Hospitalization, Illness, and Operation

Thank goodness for the medical facilities and knowledge that is available for those who need that expertise! That being said, the hospital is not the place anyone wants to stay. It is loud, noisy, uncomfortable, smelly, and full of strange viruses and bacteria. The patient rarely gets a good night's rest, and it is not uncommon that the patient hurts—a lot.

Be sensitive to time your visits according to the patient's comfort level. This is important. If you stop by the hospital without previous notice, make sure that your visit is not intruding on private family time or is not delaying medical procedures or attention. It is best to keep your visits short. The following are suggestions for serving the patient:

Bring any of the following items:

- Age-appropriate books on tape, CD, or iPod. Technology today has made it so easy to access information. iPods allow people to enjoy music, books, and instructional information at their convenience. Consider giving an iTunes card, which can be used to purchase any number of age-appropriate e-books or peaceful, relaxing music. Feel free to make suggestions! Even offer to purchase the book or music for them.

- Peaceful and relaxing music.

- A fluffy and soft animal to hold.

- A small, soft, fuzzy quilt, or lap blanket.

- Flowers (they always bring cheer).

- A potted plant in a pretty container.

- A balloon bouquet. Note: latex balloons are not allowed in the hospital. Mylar balloons are acceptable. (Save the latex balloons for when the patient is at home.)

- Special drinks, candy, or healthy snacks.

- Personal photos of animals, family, or friends of the patient.

- New, soft pajamas, slippers, or fashion socks.

- Bath gift set or personal cleaners and moisturizers.

- Attractive hair accessories.

- Useful toiletries.

- Women are usually concerned about their appearance even if they are in a hospital. Be a problem solver for this concern. This help is especially important if she must be hospitalized for a lengthy period of time. All women would agree that hair that is greasy or unkempt is depressing. Consider shampooing your friend's hair with waterless shampoo. Better still, if you have the facilities and approval of the nursing staff, shampoo with water. Be ready with a bowl, shampoo, towel, and hair dryer. This most welcome service will make all the difference in your friend's state of mind!

- Consider offering makeup for a woman if she has an extended stay. Also bring a new and attractive outfit for her to wear. This will contribute to bolstering her spirits.

Offer her some fun interactive entertainment if she is to be hospitalized for more than a few days. Consider the following:

- Play fun and relaxing board games or brainteasers.

- Consider reading to the patient when they don't have the strength or ability to read but are attentive and alert mentally.

- You could read uplifting magazine articles, short stories, novels, religious texts such as the Bible or other personal choices, or biographies.

- Share crosswords or other word puzzles.

- Spread your visits throughout the week instead of making Sunday the only day you visit. Many people make their visits on that day and weary the patient.

- Share your gift of music if you have a musical talent that can be offered in the patient's area—to the enjoyment of your friend and other patients nearby. Always get prior permission from the staff and perhaps check with the family of the patient as well. (It could be voice, flute, violin, cello, accordion, and so forth.)

- Bring a special food treat. For example, one woman was brought a strawberry milkshake after weeks in the hospital. She remembers it tasting so delicious.

It brought a welcome change from hospital food. (Of course, bringing such treats is with the assurance that the patient is not on a special diet.)

- Buy gift certificates to bookstores, video stores, or convenience stores for future needs or wants.

- Any homemade treat such as sweet rolls, breads, chocolates, or caramel popcorn is always welcome.

- When you visit, encourage the patient to talk about anything he wants to discuss. Let him know you are happy to listen. Sometimes he just wants to complain about the situation, the food, the facilities, or the nursing staff. Let him complain and be allowed to express any frustration he may feel. It is important as you are listening to him to validate his frustrations. You may say something like, "I can see how frustrating it would be," or "It must be awfully tiresome to …" Statements such as these will help him know you care and are actually interested in his situation, even though you can not do anything about the circumstances.

- Prearrange a visit from one of the patient's favorite people, such as a schoolteacher, music teacher, or mentor.

- If the patient agrees, take pictures of her progress and recovery. Present the patient with a photo album of these pictures after her release from the hospital. Including pictures of her favorite medical staff would be a nice reminder of that experience.

- Buy a new shirt or sweater for a gentleman whose hospital stay is extended.

- Consider a hand and arm or foot and lower-leg massage if the patient is in a physical condition to tolerate some touching and it isn't medically contra-indicated.

Many others besides the patient are affected by the strain of hospitalization and may be worn out. Here are some services you could provide to the doctors, nursing staff, or family:

- The medical staff always appreciates a sincere and heartfelt note of thanks for their attentions and careful nursing. These notes often are sent to the administrators of the hospital, and the staff may receive welcome recognition from their superiors.

- Bring a healthy snack or fun gifts to the nursing staff that is tending the patient.

- Volunteer to sit with the family in the lounge to keep them company if the patient is in the ICU. Be sure there is always someone with the family in the beginning stages of the experience.

- Ask a family member if they would like you to notify their spiritual/religious leader. Offer to take this individual to the hospital as needed.

- Bring a basket of healthy food and enjoyable magazines.

For extended family stays, consider the following ideas:

- Bring dinner to them on occasion.

- Consider bringing a cooler of food that can be used and refilled with the family's favorite treats or foods to sustain them during the long hours of bedside waiting.

- Help to maintain the outside appearance of their home if the stay is extended, or if the person is having alternative treatments out of town. This gives the appearance of occupancy and discourages any mischief from outsiders. It also helps maintain an attractive appearance of the home in keeping with the rest of the neighborhood.

- With their permission, do the family laundry while they are away.

- Offer to take care of their pet or pets as needed.

- Supply a notebook or journal to write down the names of visitors. Often visitors come when the patient is in a drugged stupor and unable to know or remember who visited.

- Offering personal messages of love are always welcome and can come in many forms. One family wrote a poem about their visit and gave it as a gift to the patient.

- Remember that men have a hard time being in the hospital. They need visitors also and find relaxation with a trusted friend who stops by to buoy their spirits.

- Relieve the family from the long hours of sitting and waiting. Encourage them to leave the hospital for a while as you sit with the patient in the family's absence.

- Use your time, if the patient is sleeping while you are relieving the family, to get some of your own quiet projects done, such as reading, journal writing, work projects, handwork, or homework.

- Put a poster up and have all the visitors sign it.

- Make a poster with get-well wishes of those who are not able to make it to the hospital.

- Leave a thoughtful and inspiring message on the answering machine at home for the family to listen to when they return.

- Consider taking into your home other children still at home while the parents and/or child are in the hospital, or (with a parent's permission) provide a live-in caregiver until the parents return.

- Give some money to the teenage siblings of a patient to go to dinner and a movie. The remaining children of the family feel forgotten or shuffled aside when their sibling is in the hospital getting all the attention.

- Loan your cell phone for the parents' use if they don't have one. (Note: cell phones are to be used only outside the hospital.)

Housebound or Shut-in

People may be housebound for a variety of reasons and sometimes for an extended period of time. They may not be sick but may be dealing with a myriad of physically restricting problems like a bad knee, hip, or back. They may choose to remain in the confines of their homes because it's just easier than trying to adjust to a wheelchair or walker. There are other rare but real problems such as agoraphobia, a condition in which the person simply cannot muster the courage to leave the house. Make sure you understand what is the cause for the person to be housebound and offer appropriate service to that condition.

Acts of kindness that can be offered to the housebound person helps give them the feeling that "someone cares about and remembers me." It also helps them to feel they are still a viable, valuable part of a community of friends, family, and neighbors. The following ideas can show your concern:

- Bring ability-appropriate service projects for them to do, such as tying a quilt or assembling school kits or emergency kits. (Provide the items for the kits with instructions.)

- Encourage the housebound individual to share her talents, such as woodcrafting, crocheting, or scrapbooking. Try to match a service that is needed in your community with this person's talents and offer guidance in using and/or further developing this skill. For example, crocheting leper bandages would be very useful. Another suggestion might be to knit hot pads, dishcloths, or other such items for someone else who is in need of a "gift of lift." Provide the supplies and return to pick up the finished projects.

Consider the following:

- Play fun and relaxing board games or brainteasers.

- Read uplifting magazine articles, short stories, novels, scriptures, or biographies aloud.

- Share crosswords or other word puzzles.

- Teach them skills that are appropriate for their condition, such as crocheting, knitting, or painting.

- Have them teach you one of their skills if they are physically able and appear eager to do so.

- Bring them books on tape from the library. Assess their interests and offer to keep them supplied as long as they are wanted.

- Give this person a gift certificate for an online bookstore and/or video store.

- Bring amusing audiotapes, DVDs, or CDs that are adapted to their sense of humor. (For example, Garrison Keillor, Jerry Seinfeld, Johnny Carson, *The Honeymooners*, *I Love Lucy*, etc.)

- Consider what one family did in the case of a temporarily housebound mother. This family put a bed in the living room and made that the center of activity. When meals were brought in, the children "camped out" with mom.

- Buy them a phone card so that they can stay in touch with long-distance friends and family or offer to pay their phone bill that month.

- Offer to shop for their ongoing grocery needs.

- Pick up medications as needed.

- Maintain their yard or, for a long-term situation, enlist and coordinate help on a rotating basis.

- Be prepared to do light housecleaning when necessary. Be certain this person is comfortable and accepting of this help. Be respectful of specific ways that the person wants such cleaning done.

- Buy a couple of month's worth of professional cleaning services for them.

- Do some of the laundry, with their approval. You may find this a task you can do as you are visiting. You may even decide to offer to do this on a weekly schedule, time and conditions permitting.

- Organize meals to be brought in if they can't physically keep up with the cooking. Use willing neighbors to bring in food or consider soliciting the services of community resources such as Meals on Wheels.

- Consider offering a hand and arm massage or a foot and lower-leg massage.

- Consider the person's concern for his or her animals. Offer to take them on walks or, if necessary, a groomer or veterinarian appointment.

- Water the indoor plants as needed.

- With the individual's approval, offer to clean and organize the pantry. Throw out old and forgotten items that create clutter and are not used. Reline the shelves with new paper.

- Consider giving them a manicure or pedicure, or arrange and pay for this service.

- Shampoo the person's hair. If needed, and you know how, set, perm, or color it. If not, arrange for someone to come in who does have that expertise. For men, offer to wash and/or trim their hair, or arrange to have it done.

With the individual's approval, consider the following household chores:

- Change the linens on the beds.

- Clean the carpets occasionally.

- Wash the windows as needed.

- Vacuum and dust as needed. See that this service gets done on a timely basis. (Consider enlisting young adults to take care of this on a regular schedule.)

- Remember to bring a delicious chocolate treat and offer to watch an uplifting, humorous movie with them—with or without the family!

Infertility

Many of us assume that when we want to build a family it will happen just as nature intended. A human egg is fertilized with a human sperm through intercourse, and *voila*! Nine months later a human baby is born.

Obviously, this doesn't work for everyone. One or both parents may not be capable of contributing what is necessary to create this miracle. Sometimes there simply is not a medically known reason for conception not occurring.

It can be a shattering emotional experience when a couple is informed that they are infertile. The dream and hope of having a biological child of their own has been dramatically compromised. At this point the uncertainty of whether they will ever experience parenthood feels like a dark, looming cloud that overshadows other possible parenting options. The couple feels insecure, anxious, and unsure regarding the parenting path with which they are now faced. It is so different from what they had imagined they would experience.

The emotional transition of accepting this new reality is different for each individual. Sometimes one or the other partner never accepts the situation. At other times a couple eventually comes to accept their infertile state and becomes emotionally united and ready to move forward together. Despite emotional differences that occur regarding their infertility, at some point couples can consider several parenting alternatives. Common family-building options include adoption, using a surrogate mother, or in vitro fertilization. I have chosen to highlight in vitro fertilization in this section.

Statistics show that 6.1 million Americans are infertile. That being the case, there is a vast amount of information on infertility. There were many enlightening resources

I found in researching this topic. One organization called Resolve, the National Infertility Association, stated the following: "One of the most challenging aspects of the infertility experience is dealing with the emotional ups and downs relating to medical treatment, the uncertainty about outcomes, and the challenge of having to make important decisions such as when 'enough is enough.' It is important to learn how to take care of yourself, make sure you that get the support you need, and to manage your emotions so that your self-esteem and outlook on life remains as positive as possible."[13]

Many wonderful books have been written on infertility. The available resources are too numerous to mention here. However, I would encourage anyone who wants to broaden their understanding of this pain-filled reality to use the numerous and helpful support systems that are accessible in libraries, bookstores, the Internet, magazine publications, and support groups.

Because in vitro fertilization is a complicated, stressful, and difficult experience for the woman physically, mentally, and emotionally, the following suggestions may be appropriate for her personal use. These suggestions came from women who have experienced infertility and have undergone the in vitro process.

- Find a doctor and a fertility center with which you can connect emotionally. A medical staff that you feel shares a similar philosophy and outlook regarding fertility is extremely important. The medical staff should express sensitivity to your emotions, answer your questions thoroughly, and recognize and sympathize with your pain. These are valid expectations.

- Be your own advocate. If you and/or your partner have reservations, boldly ask unanswered questions or state clearly your hesitancies until you are satisfied with the answers.

- Establish a respectful and mature relationship with your doctor.

- Get counseling or other help you may need if you are having a difficult time accepting the fact that other people have babies while you have not been so blessed. Inevitably, you will have to come in contact with other people's babies. It is vital to finally be able to face this reality without falling apart whenever you say the word baby.

- Recognize that the drugs you need for fertility will break you down emotionally. Establish a safe network of family and friends who will respond to your physical and emotional needs.

- Discuss your infertility with family or friends. It is important that you feel emotionally safe with them, as this is a very sensitive and raw subject for you. Avoid situations that may invite insensitive questions and remarks.

- Consider joining a support group. Check with your fertility clinic for reputable groups.

- Realize that it's not the end of the world if the fertility procedures don't succeed.

- Count what blessings you do have.

Continue to do simple things that give you pleasure and help to balance you emotionally. The following examples are from the American Fertility Association:

- Put flowers on your desk or at home.

- Get a massage or a pedicure.

- Go to a movie of your choice.

- Go to the theater. Something comical helps to lighten the mood.

- Keep involved with any kind of physical activity that you find satisfying. If weight gain is a problem, exercise will give you some measure of control over your body.

- Learn relaxation techniques. Deep breathing, visualization, meditation, and muscle relaxation are all great ways to calm your spirit and psyche. These disciplines will also benefit your daily life on many levels.

- Consider doing volunteer work. Serving others always makes our own problems seem less tragic.

- Consider seeing an infertility counselor or therapist if you feel your emotions are extreme and out of control.[14]

It's important to take care of yourself through trials like this. Still, help from a solid support system can make a world of difference. Following are suggestions for those who give support:

- Listen with an empathic ear. Allow your suffering friend or relative to discuss all the feelings she has at the moment. See chapter 5.

- Make sure she understands that you will be there for her whenever she has a need to talk. If there is a scheduling conflict, reschedule as soon as possible.

- Be sensitive to her ability to cope with discussing the baby topic. If she is still in an emotionally tender place, it would be better not to invite her to functions that revolve around babies such as births and baby showers.

- Refer to ideas that are listed in chapter six.

- Focus on a particular interest of hers and suggest that you pursue it together.

- Offer a spa treatment such as a pedicure, massage, or facial.

- Give her a hug and let her cry.

Remember the importance of words. The following phrases are never helpful:

"Relax; it's all in your head. Take a vacation. Then you'll get pregnant."

"Don't worry so much. It just takes time. You'll get pregnant if you're just patient."

"If you adopt a baby, you'll get pregnant."

And if you can't think of anything else, bring her a delicious chocolate treat and watch a warm, humorous movie together!

Long-Term Care—Disabilities

Long-term care is categorically well termed as a "Garden trial or Garden service." It could involve weeks, months, and sometimes years of service from the family and close, dedicated friends. This service goes far beyond dropping off a plate of cookies with a note of love and encouragement. Long-term care requires patience and a real sacrifice of time. It may be inconvenient for the giver. Following through with promises of care or fulfilling the family or patient's expectations is vital. Follow-up care is also extremely important. Each act of remembrance and support, such as the ones listed, is greatly valued.

- As with any illness, establish and maintain a trusting relationship. This may involve a testing period. The receiver may suggest small needs at first to determine if, in fact, the one serving will follow through. It is disappointing and disheartening to depend on a person for a needful act only to realize that nothing will actually get done.

Consider the ideas previously mentioned:

- Play fun and relaxing board games or brainteasers.
- Read uplifting magazine articles, short stories, novels, scriptures, or biographies aloud.

- Share crossword or other puzzles.

- Teach them skills that are appropriate for their condition: perhaps crocheting, knitting, or painting.

- Care or arrange care for the disabled person in a way that permits the family to attend Sunday services on a regular basis if possible and occasionally if not. Responsible for round-the-clock care, the family would benefit greatly from such a generous and thoughtful gesture. If the disabled person is able to attend church services, but his disability requires special care or is distracting to others, perhaps walking the halls or keeping him appropriately cared for while the meeting is in progress would be a welcome service.

- Lend a listening ear! See chapter five. Sometimes the family can be overwhelmed or frustrated by the nonstop schedule of a disabled loved one. This should not be taken as a sign that they don't want to care for the person! It was suggested to me that one should not recommend that the disabled person be placed in a home for the disabled. Allow the family to safely express their frustration. Advice is not required and not appreciated. It is recommended that you listen and try to be clear about the emotions, thoughts, and feelings of the family. Sometimes the family members just want to vent.

- Be a secret pal to the disabled for a while. Drop off goodies, small gifts, and notes of encouragement. One family experienced this with their paraplegic son. He received weekly surprises and would grin with anticipation every time the doorbell would ring. Knowing someone out there cared for him helped ease his depression and brought him much-needed joy. (The mother who encouraged this service enlisted the help of her teenage sons to drop off the weekly gifts. They were being taught the value of serving others and the satisfaction that comes with anonymous giving.)

• Make sure you follow-up on offers to help.

• Offer to take care of a pet or pet's needs, which may include veterinarian and/or grooming appointments.

• Encourage the family not to be afraid to ask for any kind of help that is needed.

• Offer to help with housekeeping chores. If you are financially able, pay for a couple of months of professional cleaning services.

One family I talked with has a twenty-year-old daughter with the mental ability of a five-year-old child. The daughter thinks that she does not need to be involved in activities and programs geared to her mental capabilities. She therefore spends most of her time at home with her parents. This is taxing on her mother, who has seven other children and is also heavily involved in her husband's business. This mother's advice to those who want to be of service in this kind of situation is for friends or neighbors to offer to include the mentally handicapped person in some of their own activities. This could include shopping, going to a movie, or other appropriate activities that keep the son or daughter occupied, interested in life, and not underfoot when other pressing family matters need to be handled.

- Value the person. Treat him or her with the respect you would give a fully-functioning friend.

- Engage in meaningful conversation. Ask questions, with genuine interest, that will allow you to get to know the person better. Resist the tendency to talk condescendingly, more slowly, or more loudly.

- Offer to spend quality one-on-one time with this individual. This will help the person with disabilities feel less lonely, and it will give you the chance to discover personality traits and talents of this person that might not be noticeable within group settings.

- Be willing to share things about yourself. Let them get to know you too. It is just as important as you getting to know them.

- Consider offering a hand and/or arm massage. Maybe a foot and/or lower-leg massage would be appreciated as well.

- Show love with action. Do little things—a smile, a note, a telephone call. Or extend an invitation to a luncheon, a party, or an evening event. These can make all the difference in their ability to persevere in their affliction.

- If you are unsure about the condition of the individual, ask direct and clear questions about the disability. This understanding will help you know better how to serve this unique individual.

- Consider sewing themed pillow-covers for the cushion of the seat of a wheelchair that is used regularly.

- Invite the disabled person to go to parties with you, on a visit to another person who needs comfort, or just to visit. Be available or arrange for the needed transportation. Remember to take them home before they get too tired, even if the activity is not over.

- Encourage a young man or young woman to help prepare clothing, dress, and transport the disabled person to meetings, appointments, or other activities.

- Offer to give the parents of a disabled person a night out. This loving service is especially helpful during the holidays.

- Get creative and bring a chocolate treat to eat and a warm, humorous movie to watch! (This could be very helpful for the primary caregiver!)

Miscarriage

A miscarriage of an acknowledged pregnancy is a very sad event for a woman. The woman who has experienced miscarriage seldom discloses it. The quiet loss is poignant and painful, accompanied by heart-wrenching emotions, especially for the woman. Often her partner shares these heavy-hearted feelings.

According to the March of Dimes, a miscarriage is defined as "a pregnancy loss that occurs before twenty weeks, before the fetus is able to survive outside the womb. Most miscarriages occur in the first trimester or twelve weeks of pregnancy. A miscarriage can be an intensely sad and frightening experience. A pregnancy that had seemed normal suddenly ends, leaving expectant parents devastated. About 15 percent of recognized pregnancies end this way."[15]

A friend of mine described it as a "loss of a dream." That aptly described the common explanations I heard from many women I questioned regarding miscarriages that they had experienced. With joyful expectation, recognizing that a lovely, warm bundle was growing inside of her, the woman forms a bond with the fetus early in pregnancy. This bond develops each day, and often the mother naturally anticipates the child's future and all the wonderful interactions she is going to have. She may even give the fetus a nickname, which she and her partner playfully refer to during the ensuing months of growth. She expects an armful of soft, responsive warmth to nurture and cuddle at the end of gestation. Suddenly, it's over! The dream, the hope, has been shattered.

I recall a very good friend of mine who miscarried at about four months. She collected the fetus in a plastic bag as the doctor had instructed. Before she went to her appointment, she showed it to me. As I looked upon this very miniscule human body, I realized the importance of this fetus to my friend. She had named her, she had often talked about her, and she deeply mourned her loss. I remember feeling acutely inadequate in knowing how to comfort her.

The Grief Process: What should I expect?

The grieving process involves three steps:

Step 1: Shock/Denial. "This really isn't happening. I've been taking good care of myself."

Step 2: Anger/Guilt/Depression. "Why me? If I would have . . ." "I've always wanted a baby so badly, this isn't fair. I feel more sadness in my life now more than ever."

Step 3: Acceptance. "I have to deal with it. I'm not the only one who has experienced this. Other women have made it through this, maybe I should get some help."

"Each step takes longer to go through than the previous one. There are unexpected and sometimes-anticipated triggers that lead to setbacks. Examples of potential triggers include: baby showers, birth experience stories, new babies, OB/GYN office visits, nursing mothers, thoughtless comments, holidays, and family reunions.

"When we offer help to someone through this time, they are often in such shock they don't know what they need. The objectives are to encourage the venting of her grief and reestablishing her self-esteem while recognizing her sorrow. Whatever the person is feeling, they deserve to have their feelings supported by the people around them."

The following suggestions from HopeXchange are particularly helpful:

- Contact is important. Be there if possible, but if not, ring or write.

- A hug or arm around her shoulders is comforting.

- Understand that her tears are a healthy response and should never be discouraged. Having a box of tissues handy is helpful.

- Let her do the talking. Be the passive partner who asks questions and focus on certain points to help her talk about her feelings. It is sufficient to just listen.

- Tell her how you feel about her losing the baby and how sorry you are.

- Acknowledge her pain even if you think you would not react this way in this situation.

- Ask questions about her experience, how she is really feeling, and what she is thinking about.

- Encourage her to be patient and not to impose "shoulds" on herself. Grieving takes time.

- Reassure her that she did everything she could and it wasn't her fault. It helps alleviate her guilt.

- Grieving is a physically exhausting process, and she will probably need to sleep or rest during the day.

Take whatever steps necessary to give her the unin-
terrupted peace to do this.

- The intensity of grief fluctuates. During less tearful
  times, a change of scenery is appreciated.

- Do something practical such as shopping or taking
  around a meal.

- Put on soothing music for her to listen to, offer a
  back massage, or a walk on the beach. When she
  feels ready, take her to a movie of her choice.

- If you are seriously worried about her behavior,
  seek professional advice. As a rule of thumb, as long
  as she is not damaging herself, another person, or
  property, you probably don't have anything to worry
  about.

Refer to chapter 6 for many other positive suggestions
to support and comfort. As always, along with the many
ways you can help, be sure to avoid the following hurtful
actions:

- Don't ignore her because you feel helpless or
  uncomfortable with grief. She will wonder if what
  happened to her means nothing to you.

- Don't think that miscarriage is easier to cope with
  than a stillbirth or neonatal death. The truth is that
  her baby has just died, and it doesn't really matter
  how pregnant she was.

- Don't be anxious or embarrassed about making her

cry. It is not what you said or did that upset her, but losing the baby. By allowing her to cry, you are helping her work through the process of grief.

- Don't confuse support with cheering her up. Grief is an enormously powerful emotion and needs releasing, not repressing.

- Don't put on a bright cheery front yourself.

- Don't assume there will be another pregnancy.

- Don't try to do all the housework. Although well intentioned, she needs to feel capable and useful.

- Don't forget, her children have lost a sibling, and it is natural for them to react in some way.

- Don't feel guilty if you're pregnant. Just forgive her if she's cold and withdrawn. It's her way of coping.

- Don't feel you have to keep your children away. She must go through the process of accepting others' children.

- Don't ask how she is feeling if you only do so as a social obligation. It obliges you to listen carefully to the complete answer.

Seven helpful things to say:

- "I'm so sorry about your miscarriage."
- "I know how much you wanted that baby."
- "It's okay to cry."
- "Can I call you back next week to see how you are doing?"
- "I was wondering how you are feeling about your miscarriage now."

- "I don't really know what to say."
- "It must be so awful for you after going through those weeks of IVF treatment to have lost your baby."

Seven Things *not* to say:

- "You can always have another one."

- "There was probably something wrong with it. It's nature's way."

- "It's God's will."

- "At least you didn't know the baby. It would have been much worse if it had happened later."

- "I know how you feel."

- "It wasn't really a baby yet."

- "You're young; there's plenty of time. If you stop focusing on being pregnant so much, it will just happen."

If in doubt, say something—anything—and be prepared to listen. Possibly the hardest thing, even harder than hearing an insensitive comment, is when people say nothing at all[16].

- Bring your friend a delicious chocolate treat and share an uplifting, humorous girl movie together as soon as you feel it is appropriate!

Moving Day

Has anyone not experienced a move? Yuck! Even though this list is a bit short, because we all have gone through this exhausting and taxing time, I suspect each of us can come up with one or two ideas that may not be listed here. Personalize your offerings based on what you found to be helpful in your moves. There is no way around it—it is 100 percent physically and emotionally draining. Preparation, packing, and unpacking always take more time than one thinks, and often time runs out before everything is done. So offer your muscles and a smile. Anything is appreciated!

- One person advised, making sure that the person or family that is moving actually wants help before offering. Some people don't want or need the extra hands.

- Find out specifically what kind of help is needed. Ask directly. If the answer is a weary and vague reply or simply "I don't know," look around, see the obvious, and then jump in and do the work.

- Offer to help do some preliminary packing if you know in advance when they are moving. There are numerous miscellaneous items that can be packed well before moving day.

- Offer to help do anything. Bring drinks, tend the children, and if there is enough muscle power, help unpack or pack boxes, set up beds, and so forth.

- Arriving with food is always appreciated. This is especially true if the power has been turned off. If it is summertime, bring cold drinks, sandwiches, and fruit. If it is in the wintertime, hot chocolate and soup are great comfort foods.

- Put new liners in closets, drawers, or the pantry.

- Help collect boxes and packing material before moving day.

- Help move closet clothes by rubber banding the handles of the hangers together (if the move is local).

- Clean closets/drawers after they are emptied.

- Help clean the house after everything has been moved out.

- Make time at the end of the day to share a yummy chocolate treat (hot chocolate in the winter and chocolate ice cream in the summer) and a warm, humorous movie, and hope everyone can stay awake until the end!

New Area

This category could have been put under "Moving Day," but I felt it needed to be a separate listing. Moving into a new neighborhood, let alone a whole new area where the unfamiliar looms large, is overwhelming to say the least! If someone does not have a network of family or friends in the area, getting settled can be intimidating. Here are some ideas that may help the transition go more smoothly for the individual or the family:

- Volunteer (as an individual or as a group) to clean and prepare the house to receive the furniture. This service was done by a group of volunteers for a family with a recently built house. It was a large project!

They went in and cleaned up all the construction mess inside the house so the family could bring in their personal effects on a timely schedule. It is a service that is usually paid for, but this group of neighbors wanted to do it without pay and did so in two-and-a-half hours!

- Find out what day the family is moving in and bring in dinner for the first couple of nights.

- Pay an initial visit within a day or two of your new neighbor's arrival. Give them friendly and uplifting information about the area and the neighbors.

- Offer to take them to cultural, community, or church activities until they have met a few people and are comfortable going on their own.

- A homemade loaf of bread with a friendly welcome note is always appreciated. Take along some jam, honey, or butter also.

- Make a list of professionals in the area that are highly recommended. Include doctors, dentists, salons (hair and nails), schools, daycare, music teachers, nurseries (for the yard), and numbers of churches. Also helpful are the numbers to city hall, the police, animal services, and other community services.

- Children of a similar age could help make cookies and take a plate over to their new friend.

- Lend extra hands to help move the furniture into the home.

- Offer to tend the children during moving day.

- Take over food and drinks for the laborers.

- Set up the bed frames first and then put on the bedding.

- Help unpack and organize the kitchen.

- Break down the packing boxes and paper used. Offer to take them to the recycling center within a day or two of the move-in. They take up enormous space and contribute to the sense of chaos and disarray.

- Bring them a delicious chocolate treat and a humorous movie for them to watch—when all is settled!

New Baby—Adoption/Natural

I remember being in a class about motherhood that was taught by a mother of eight. She expressed the idea that the first two weeks of a child's life is the sweetest time for a mother and child to have together. She stated that this was the time when a woman feels as close to heaven as she will ever experience. I recall understanding and agreeing with this sentiment completely.

There has been nothing in my life to compare with the supreme bliss and contentment of those first couple of weeks. Ah, babies! I videotaped two of my three children's births, and each time I watch them I am immediately transported back to that day that was filled with wonder, joy, gratitude, and bliss. I am a changed woman forever. This category is one of the few listed in this book that offers potential for joy and wonder.

However, sometimes there can be physical defects with the baby that may or may not be expected upon delivery. The parents' initial realization is one of the most difficult with which to cope. It is rather heartbreaking, as a parent, to accept the fact that your baby has physical challenges and difficulties that affect and change the scope of the baby's life as well as your own. One woman said that when she was told her child had PKU (a disease in which the body is unable to break down and metabolize the amino acid phenylalanine), she withdrew from social contact. She needed time to cry. It was necessary for her to have space and time to process this change in her circumstances and deal with her grief and pain. She understood people's desires to want to visit with her or assist her as she adjusted to being a new mother. But it was important for her to be in a quiet place with herself and her baby, alone. Once she felt strong enough to cope with her new realities, she was in a better place emotionally to accept the kindnesses of others. Respecting the privacy of a new mother under any kind of circumstances is thoughtful and welcomed.

Sometimes the circumstances can be as simple as all went well, there are no issues or challenges of any kind, and mother and child are great. Sometimes the newborn circumstances resulted because of the wonderful option of adoption. People can forget that even though a woman has not given birth to her newly-adopted child, her needs, as well as her family's needs, are similar to mothers who have given birth. Be sensitive to adoption situations and offer to help them with any of the following ideas. Each of these ideas can certainly ease the initial load of any new mother, one who has given birth or one who has an adopted infant or child.

- Always call before stopping by!

- Take a basket of healthy snack foods, a magazine, lotion, powder, lip balm, some calming music, or a favorite drink for the mother.

- Offer to take younger siblings to a park, to your home, or out shopping (if you are brave enough!).

- Offer to take a younger sibling or siblings to your home to play with your children once a week for a couple of hours for a month.

- Bring a humorous book to the new mother.

- Offer to watch the baby as you give the new mother an opportunity to take a much-needed nap.

- Bring her favorite treat.

- Leave your little children at your home when you visit.

- Consider offering a hand and arm massage, or a foot and lower-leg massage (as with other categories that center on physical recovery).

- Bring a meal! They are always appreciated—especially between two and four weeks later. See the section called "Let's Talk Food" in chapter 6.

- Send a card or an encouraging note with a fun quote.

- Give a subscription to a diaper service if you are in the financial position. Check with the mother to make sure she wants to use cotton diapers.

- If the above offering is declined, how about giving her a few months worth of housecleaning services?

- If the baby is bottle-fed and your friendship with the mother is one of shared trust and confidence, offer to spend the night and take care of the feeding times, which allows the mother to get at least one full night of sleep!

- Consider offering to run to the store for items she may need.

- Take her out to lunch if she feels that she can get away.

- Plan on spending time just listening—see chapter five.

- Never give advice (unless it is asked for)!

- Offer to help with the laundry. It may be greatly appreciated. One new body in the house seems to triple the laundry load. Consider taking it to your own home to get it done so that you are not underfoot at the new mother's house.

- Offer to do a little house cleaning. Two extra hands are always helpful.

- Pay for a professional house-cleaning service for a month or two if funds allow.

- Take some time with a new mother and help her with the basics of baby care if she has no family in the area.

- Check in with a new teenage mom after a couple of weeks and assess her needs. She probably could use a break from the constancy of motherhood, especially since it is so drastic a change from her previous activities.

- Find community resources that would be helpful for a young mother and encourage her to get involved. Go with her to the first few meetings until she feels comfortable with the support group.

- Schedule a Friday evening several weeks after the baby arrives where you will bring in dinner for the husband and wife as a date-night dinner. Arrange for the other children to be tended, have the meal prepared, set the table with china, candles, and nice silverware. Play romantic or quiet music in the background.

- Offer to attend to the mother's civic or church responsibilities for a month or two, until she is feeling more balanced.

- Focus on the mother and her baby for this visit. I strongly suggest that you stay clear of discussing your own birthing experiences or war stories from other women.

"Preemies"

The experience of delivering a premature baby is filled with anxiety, stress, and hand wringing. It is so difficult for the parents to leave their child in the hospital when they want desperately to take their baby home with them! Obviously, if that infant survives and can be taken home, the wait will have been worth all the fretfulness and worry. Perhaps the appreciation of that newborn is even more poignant. Love, support, and encouragement from neighbors, friends, and family are all highly valued by the parents. When the family is again reunited at home, the following ideas can be especially helpful.

- Refer to the category "Hospitalization" for ideas that will help with supporting the family during the baby's initial time in NICU.

- Offer to drive her to the hospital if she is still recovering from a particularly difficult delivery and needs someone to assist her in this way.

- Check in with the husband to assess how best to help him with the household chores or children when his wife is at the hospital. Some men need a lot of help while others are pretty self-sufficient and would prefer taking care of the family on their own.

- Show up and offer to listen. (Refer to chapter 5.) This is a very emotional time for the mother. Hormones are raging through the body. She is trying to cope emotionally without her baby at home. She may need to have a sympathetic ear in which to vent and a strong shoulder on which to cry or laugh.

- Help do some of the housework that is not getting done. Clean up the kitchen, do the laundry, or fold and put away clothes as you can. Vacuum, dust, straighten up clutter, and put toys away. All these are helpful services that will be noticed and appreciated.

- Offer to tend the other children when the mother goes to the hospital to visit or nurse her baby.

Parenting (Step-parenting, Foster Care, Single Parenting)

I include parenting as one of the service categories because of the many difficult issues that come with being a parent. Extra help or comfort may be very much appreciated at times. Nobody is prepared for being a parent. It does not matter how the children come, whether naturally or through adoption.

Parenting is a daunting, overwhelming responsibility that requires attention to detail and growing through numerous changes, all while trying to cope with life. Parenting gets even more complicated when families are blended, producing a step-parenting situation. If you are involved in foster care with children who are not your own or you become a single parent, you find yourself in stressful situations at best! Every parent, in whatever parental situation, will at some point cry, "Help!"

It is comforting to know that this club of mothers and fathers is bound together by a clear understanding of just how difficult it is to be a parent, let alone an effective one. Some families have extremely harsh, difficult, and upsetting circumstances that never seem to go away. Other homes have normal day-to-day crises that parents are generally capable of handling. And then there are some homes that hum along as the parents gently oversee their kids with very little head-butting between generations. Whichever is the case for you or those you know, be on the alert to give some stressed-out parent their own version of time out.

For step-parenting, refer to chapter 6. Many of these ideas are great to implement for an overworked and stressed-out parent in an awkward half role. Those ideas, along with some of the following can also be extremely helpful for single parents. One single parent inspired me by her service despite a very taxing situation.

I met Helen because she was recommended as a woman who intimately understands service. Helen is seventy-two years old, very young at heart, and a delightful and playful individual. After raising three children of her own, Helen has found herself parenting again, but this time as a single parent. She was widowed for the second time in 2004. She has two grandsons, ages five and nine. Besides the fact that they are young and busy as boys will be, the oldest child also has autism, which requires greater attention and time. Helen is also heavily involved in community humanitarian work. This work consumes many hours of labor as she organizes workdays, interfaces with the volunteers, and distributes the kits, quilts, and other goods that are donated and assembled to charitable organizations.

My point in highlighting Helen's situation is that other people's choices can and do affect our reality. Helen did not think she would be a hands-on parent again at this stage in her life, and she certainly didn't count on being a single parent. She is an inspiration to observe as she continues to be highly involved in her life's passion—serving others, while at the same time being a single parent! Because single parents can be so overwhelmed, they can always use some of the following services:

- Organize a teenage work force to help with outside yard work as needed.

- Relieve the constancy of someone who is single parenting by helping to tend the children. It could be done on a weekly or monthly basis, or as you have time.

- Have a group of young people clean, organize, and put away the toys every once in a while.

- Offer to help with the handyman tasks that go with maintaining a house. Change lights or fix problems with the plumbing, water softener, hot water heater, or shingles on the roof.

- Offer to clean up the yard. You could mow the lawn, rake leaves, tend to the flowerbeds, or weed.

- Consider washing the windows inside and out a couple of times a year.

- Make a date with your friend and take her to dinner and a movie or lunch and a matinee. Similarly, go to the theater or a concert.

For foster parents, the strain can be of a different nature. Consider some of the ideas in chapter 6. You could also try the following:

- Help raise money for the sponsoring family to alleviate financial strains that may occur.

- Shop garage sales and pick up toys for the children or other useful items.

- Help foster parents maintain their yard, repair broken household items, or work on projects around the home.

- Assess any special needs that involve the children. In discovering such needs, connect the family with appropriate support groups or agencies. (See "Long-term Care" for other ideas.)

- Okay, let's hear it for some chocolate treats and a warm, funny movie right about now!

Pet Loss

Pets are often a very large part of a family's or an individual's life. To illustrate this point, recall all the pets that were left behind by their owners in their flight of survival from hurricane Katrina. There were thousands of pets rescued and placed in shelters waiting to be reclaimed. Many of the owners were heartbroken as they were forced to leave their pet behind. There were many happy stories of reunion that serve to reinforce the fact that pets are a huge part of some people's lives.

There are also dozens of stories of extraordinary animals that find their way back to their owners after being abandoned or lost. Heartwarming movies about the love, bond, and experiences between an animal and its owner usually guarantee tears of satisfaction if the story ends happily, or often tears of sadness as deep feelings of understanding and empathy are felt if the story ends in loss. Either way, animals and their relationship with the human family have a huge impact on our emotional state. When there is pet-loss, it can be a devastating experience.

Sometimes a pet is the family for an individual. The relationship that is built between a pet and its owner is extremely personal; it is one that is built on love, trust, and companionship. When the animal is suffering physically and all the medical help has run its course, the best thing to do is to relieve the pet's suffering by having it put down. However, this decision is very difficult for the owner to make and to accept, let alone to see through. If the pet's life is taken in an accident, the painful emotional repercussions for the owners are acute.

The following story is a very poignant example of love and loss for one young lady. Kelly was ten when she received Tyana, a beautiful Paint horse trained for roping, steering, and jumping competitions. Many of the skills required in competition are dangerous, with precise timing expected to enable correct execution of the skills without injury to horse or rider. Kelly and Tyana learned to rely on the intricate timing they developed together. This daily practice of skill execution established a deep relationship of trust and connection between them.

One day after riding Tyana, Kelly brushed her, gave her an apple, and said goodbye. That evening Tyana's trainer called with the news that Tyana had died. The horse had experienced extreme colic after eating the apple. Her abdomen had become twisted and then had ruptured, causing death within two hours.

Her mother received the news, feeling shock and grief,

knowing how much Kelly adored this horse. She conveyed the news to Kelly as gently as she could and held her daughter tightly. During the next couple of days, she listened to all the grief and pain Kelly was able to express. Once Kelly was feeling strong enough to return to school, she found it difficult to relate to the stories of compassion that her friends shared with her on their loss of their dog or cat. She reasoned a relationship with a dog or cat is nothing like the relationship she had with her horse, Tyana. Her experience was much more emotionally shattering because of the depth of their bond, which was developed while roping, jumping, and working together every day. A oneness was developed and a dependency created that she didn't feel her friends could form with a typical domestic dog or cat. It was a very difficult period for Kelly.

Six weeks later, Kelly's parents purchased her another horse. Snip was not the same as Tyana, and Kelly had a hard time making this adjustment to another animal. However, a relationship was formed with satisfying results, personally and professionally. Throughout the next five years, Kelly won fifteen World Buckles, the Youth World Championship and Hi Point English Championship in 2002, as well as the Number One Youth in the Nation for the Year 2002 on the new horse. Recovery from personal pet loss does happen. However, the process is slow and painful and often we don't understand why our beloved animal is gone.

Sometimes the loss of a pet is not death. Perhaps the animal has run away or been stolen. Find out the details and contribute your help if there are solutions to the loss.

Many organizations are set up to help retrieve pets that are misplaced or lost during disasters. Consider some of the following suggestions to ease the pet owner's pain:

- A phone call expressing your sympathy is always appreciated.

- Awareness by friends of the ache one suffers at the loss of a beloved pet is important. One woman saw an acquaintance at the veterinarian's office with her cat that needed to be put down. She made a phone call to another friend who was on more familiar terms with this acquaintance and relayed the news of this woman's pet loss. That friend took a plate of cookies and an "I'm thinking of you" visit to the bereaved pet owner.

- Consider donating a small amount of money to the family if they are planning to put a headstone on their pet's grave.

- Offer to drive them to the veterinarian's office if they are going to put their pet down. Or, if they feel they are not emotionally strong enough to take their pet to the veterinarian's office, offer to do so for them.

- Buy a small plant or tree for their yard in remembrance of their pet.

- Give fresh flowers with an uplifting note.

- Take them to lunch and let them talk about their animal. Ask questions about their pet. Take an interest in their answers.

- Visit a pet store or animal section of a department store and find an appropriate wall hanging, plaque, or framed saying that would be a reminder of their pet and of the joy their pet brought to them.

- If you have the inclination and money, consider an ad in a newspaper or trade magazine if the pet was an exceptional animal. As in the case of Kelly and Tyana, her mother paid for a one-page ad in the *Paint Horse Journal* to honor the horse and explain the incident of loss to the people who knew the family, followed Kelly's accomplishments, and were concerned for Kelly.

- Bring a wonderful chocolate treat and spend an evening watching a humorous movie with your friend. (I wouldn't recommend movies like *Old Yeller* or *Where the Red Fern Grows!*)

Recuperating after Surgery, Injury, or Illness

The process after an illness, injury, or surgery is often long, pain-filled, and lonely. It is a time that requires patience of the giver and the receiver. Sometimes family and friends expect recovery and progress to be faster than it actually is. Clear communication between the patient and their loved ones is important. Being too emotionally sensitive is tempting. For everyone involved, it is best to remember not to take comments and conversations too personally. Feelings can be unintentionally hurt. It is important to remember that careful listening and clear understanding of what a recuperating person needs, wants, or expects be made plain for all parties concerned. Keep these ideas in mind:

- Establish a trusting relationship with the recuperating person over a period of time. This could be seen as a testing period. The receiver may suggest small needs at first to determine if you will in fact follow through.

- Offer to tend the children for a couple of hours once a week, or as you can. If there is a more frequent need, put together a list of individuals who would be willing to help tend at such times. Organize the volunteers into hours and days as needed.

- When you visit, something as simple as fluffing their pillows and straightening the sheets and blankets is helpful.

- Refill their water pitcher with fresh water and ice.

- Bring them healthy snacks that are appropriate to their recommended diet.

- Visit and listen. Remember to keep the visit short and sincere. Refer to chapter 5 for detailed suggestions on effective listening.

- Visit with the family members of the patient while he or she is napping or otherwise occupied. These family members can feel neglected while serving and tending to the person requiring care.

- Offer your home, if circumstances allow, in situations in which surgery and the recuperation period have been more extensive than expected. This may arise if the family is unable or elderly.

- Offer the use of essential oils and herbs if you have knowledge and experience in their use and you believe the oils would be helpful in the recuperative process.

- Offer to get some shopping done for the family. This could include groceries, household goods, school clothes, or other items.

- Be a chauffer for the children if the parent or parents are recuperating from illness or surgery.

- Be aware of house-cleaning chores that need to be done. Consider hiring a professional house-cleaning service if there are funds available, or ask for willing volunteers to help you. Such needs may be expected once a week for a couple of months or only a week or two.

- Gain permission to do outside yard work if it needs attention. Enlist teenagers in the neighborhood to help with this task.

- Attend to any house maintenance that is needed. Ask pointed questions about repair work. Get it done quickly.

- Bring a delicious chocolate treat for the patient and family, along with a humorous movie to watch when the time is right.

Suicide

It is said that the family of the suicide victim often feels some degree of guilt after the suicide. The feeling of culpability greatly increases their personal suffering and anguish. Those who want to help can feel stymied about what to do, how and when to help, and what is appropriate for this sensitive period of time.

There are many articles available that will help you know how to comfort or help the family of the suicide victim. These sources are useful in gaining a clearer understanding of the family's emotional agony. It will increase your own understanding and ability to better comfort and serve them. Other ideas follow:

- Contact 911. This alerts the authorities, police, and paramedics to begin the necessary paperwork that needs to be filed.

- Take charge cleaning the area where the death occurred. Do your best to erase any physical signs of what happened.

- Contact the local clergy with which the family has a relationship. If there is no such relationship, ask the family if they would like you to get someone whom you trust to provide this assistance.

- Contact immediate family members. Assist them in any way you perceive a need.

- Provide food. Though on the initial day little thought will be given to eating, nourishment will help to sustain the family's strength for the tasks that need to be done.

- See the "Funeral" category for other suggestions that might be appropriate for this situation.

- Encourage the survivors to write a letter to the loved one that took his or her life. This will help them release the feelings they may not have had the chance to express. Hanging on to guilt, confusion, or anger is not healthy for their own spirits. They need an outlet for expression. A letter could be a positive step toward their emotional healing.

- Be sensitive to offhand comments such as "I would rather kill myself," or "I would die if I had to do that," or "Take a flying leap." These trite phrases can be said flippantly with little thought to their impact if said in the company of one who has experienced the suicide of a loved one.

  Never say anything like:

  "Oh no, not your brother! I had no idea he was that messed up!"

  "How did he take his life?"

  "Did you find him?"

  "What did he look like?"

  "Was there anything you did to drive him to it?"

- Bring a mouth-watering chocolate treat when things have calmed down a bit. Don't forget a warm, uplifting movie. (This is a time-and case-sensitive suggestion, but it may help.)

Unemployment

When someone loses his or her job through downsizing, outsourcing, layoffs, firing, or a territory or factory closing, it feels as though the world has collapsed. The road needed to pay the monthly expenses and obligations is closed. It is a shock to realize the anchor of security has just been cut. One's sense of self-reliance, independence, and even self-worth plummets, fueling insecurity about the future, as well as how to make ends meet from day to day. Some people may look at this as an opportunity for new adventures. Others can feel their life has come to an abrupt end. Whatever attitude you may encounter with someone who is unemployed, initially it can be an uncomfortable experience for you when you help out. Especially if you sense or know they are embarrassed. Stay with the intention of easing their way, but be sensitive in your approach.

After twenty-one years of being a stay-at-home mom, I became a single woman again. I soon realized that I needed to find employment to sustain myself. What I experienced was months of unsuccessful job hunting. It dawned on me that I had great skill sets that were about twenty-five years old. It was discouraging knowing I had the ability to be successful in many of the jobs that I applied for, but was unable to secure initial interviews because after reading my resume it was obvious I had been out of the workforce for a number of years. No one was willing to gamble on my rusty skills.

I found that the support I received from family and friends during this time contributed to my confidence in knowing that I would eventually become employed. The support was consistent with many of the suggestions that are listed here. The following ideas may help sustain the hope that there is light at the end of the unemployment tunnel:

- Present them with a "Job-loss Survival Kit." The kit may include any of the following: movies, oversized sunglasses, or a great book to read. Suggest they take time to lounge in the backyard or indulge in the time they have to watch their favorite movies. A few books to consider: *All Creatures Great and Small*, by James Herriott; *Byzantium*, by Steven Lawhead; *A Year in Provence*, by Peter Mayle; *The Education of Little Tree*, by Forrest Carter; *The Robe*, by Lloyd Douglas; *The Great Gatsby*, by F. Scott Fitzgerald; *A Girl of the Limberlost*, by Gene Stratton-Porter.

- Encourage them to keep at the search. It is a rough experience for them because rejection is common until there is a fit between their talents and a job.

- Have them consider temporary work if that is an option.

- Offer support. Listen. Let the person vent. Refer to chapter 5.

- Drop off treats and/or meals anonymously.

- Discuss with them the possible benefit of a new résumé. If you are proficient and know what you are doing, offer to help them; if you are not, find and suggest an appropriate resource and support.

- Avoid saying anything respecting material assets, such as, "Oh, don't worry; look at the diamond ring you are wearing!" or "Look at the beautiful cars you are driving!" or "What are you worried about? You have a great house in which to live." Comments such as these are hurtful. These possessions do not reflect the dire financial needs of the family.

- Consider sending flowers or a plant with a note attached. In the note offer encouraging words. Also consider sending money. Any amount is helpful, whether it is five dollars or fifty! (This could be done anonymously.) The need is great!

- Offer to accompany the head or heads of the family on that first journey to collect welfare food if the family is at that point of need. Such support and love may be very much appreciated at that difficult time.

- As in my case, my girlfriend offered me free room and board, open ended, until my needs shifted. It was a life saver!

- Consider purchasing a few sacks full of groceries and anonymously leaving them on their front door step. Make sure to drop it off when you know some-one is at home and will retrieve the food promptly. A disguised and anonymous phone call would be helpful!

- Inform them of any job leads of which you become aware. Use the contacts you have and network for them if it is appropriate and possible.

- If there is an opportunity, encourage them to get involved in a volunteer organization or engage in simple acts of kindness themselves.

- An evening of chocolate decadence and a funny movie is a great escape!

- Once a new job is secured, celebrate with more chocolate decadence and another funny movie!

Wedding/Reception

Though I have not to this point in time been responsible for the details of a wedding or reception, I know many people who have experienced the stress and strain of preparing for such an event. From an outsider's point of view, the list of things to do seems unbelievably long and tedious, yet it is just that attention to detail that makes the event so rewarding and memorable. As I have gingerly offered my help on occasion, I have been amply rewarded with great appreciation from my worn-out friends. These suggestions are from veterans of this happy yet stressful time.

- Come with a specific offer to help. This will give you control over what you would like to be in charge of.

- Take food to the family the day before the wedding. Be sure it is nourishing, strengthening, and healthy.

It will help keep their energy up for the seemingly endless list of things to accomplish.

- Share your wedding props and extra supplies with others to help them keep expenses down.

- Offer kitchen help during the reception.

- Offer clean-up help after the reception. Not many people stay for this part of the fun.

- Offer your home to your friend's out-of-town friends and family.

- Just show up and say, "I'm available."

- Go to the reception as an invited guest. This is a tender time for families, especially the parents of the bride and groom, and they want to share in their happiness while celebrating their child's joy.

- Get a card container for those cards that come without a present. This helps to prevent a loss. If you are in charge of the gift table, make sure the cards are taped to the present they come with, which prevents the "lost card disaster." When the reception is over, take the gifts to the appropriate location for the bride and groom to open at their disposal.

- If the wedding ceremony is a private occasion, offer to help tend small children of relatives during the ceremony.

- If the ceremony is performed in a private residence, consider taking a home video if there is no professional photographer.

- Tending the children of out-of-town guests is appreciated when an activity for the family is adult only.

- Celebrate the success of a party well thrown with a delicious chocolate treat and a great, humorous movie on a night other than the reception!

Widow—Widower

My dearest friend lost her husband and soul mate in the prime of her life. There had been such promise for a wholesome, happy, and successful future. They were deeply content with the richness of their relationship. His unexpected passing left her shaken to the core, barely able to breathe, trying to make sense of the loss as she struggled to cope with day-to-day activities. Observing her experience has helped me realize what a gut-wrenching void is created with this loss.

Despite the fact that millions of people have experienced the same loss, the journey to a wholeness of sorts is a solo one. However, we can do a lot to assist and support their recovery. Having an understanding of the grieving process is important. Refer to chapter four to gain some clarity and basic insight to the general grieving cycle.

Individuals who are suddenly shocked into a reality that doesn't include their spouse are often unable to think logically or practically. Should you come to their door ready to help but without a specific task in mind, they may likely be unable or unwilling to give out assignments. If they are not receptive now to your offer to help, leave graciously and try again later. Here are some suggestions:

- Come prepared with a specific act of kindness in mind. Assess obvious needs and take the appropriate action.

- Acknowledge the death of the spouse. Acknowledge the impact of the loss for the surviving spouse. Ignoring the fact of the beloved's death is unsympathetic, unkind, and cold. Several widows emphasized this sentiment.

- Keep the acknowledgement short and sincere: "I'm sorry for your loss."

- Be sensitive to the cycle of healing. If you have a comfortable relationship with this person, call during the depression stage (weeks or even months later) and offer your love, encouragement, and a listening ear.

- Be careful not to let the person feel like the local charity project. It creates a sense of finality they are not ready to embrace. You can avoid this by being personable, loving, willing, and available.

- Food is always helpful. Suggest that they consider eating at a different table than the one they shared with their spouse, if they have a choice.

- Very tactfully suggest they consider the purchase of a different bed and that a smaller one may work better. This suggestion is conditional on how close your relationship is and if there are means available.

- Offer to take this friend to social situations. Now single, she may feel awkward when there are other couples at these settings. She is more comfortable with the familiarity of friends and enjoying comfortable companionship. In her mind and heart, she is still processing the emotional adjustment and acceptance of being a single person.

- Money is very helpful. Insurance money may take several months or longer to reach the family. Meanwhile, immediate expenses accumulate.

- Take your newly single friend on a date. Go out for a milkshake, a walk, or a short drive. Evenings are particularly difficult and lonely.

- Let your friend talk. Listen! (Refer to chapter 5.)

- Sometimes the individual simply doesn't want to talk or interact. Respect their need for silence and personal grieving time.

- Plant a couple of pots with bright-colored annuals while they are at the funeral. Keep the pots replanted each year on the anniversary of the death.

- Never say, "Just wait, it gets worse." (I know it seems obvious, but one woman was given this cold and insensitive comment shortly after her husband died!)

- Engage a crew of people to help you organize, prepare the soil, and plant the seeds of a vegetable garden for one who is used to having a garden. Make sure your friend has the energy to maintain the garden. If not, be prepared to maintain the garden as needed or find willing individuals who want to help with this service.

- Hugs are always appreciated.

- If the widow/widower is a young parent, often what is missed most are the date nights away from the children when the adults can talk. Present him or her with an opportunity for a date with you and allow all the time needed to discuss important issues and brag about what the children are doing. Allow your friend to laugh and cry as needed.

- Keep in touch on a regular basis. Send notes and/or cards of encouragement, make regular, uplifting phone calls, or send them cheerful e-mails.

- Set up a weekly lunch date, either in or out of your home. If the friend does not feel like venturing out yet, bring lunch in once a week. The connection with a friend and the consistency of the appointment are very important. This activity is something to look forward to, as well as momentarily being a distraction from the painful loss.

- Remember birthdays and holidays with a call and a cheerful card.

- Try to time your calls at lonely times of the days and weeks, usually during the evenings and weekends. Remember, this time of day could also be a difficult time for them to want to talk. Be sensitive to the individual's emotional needs. When I call my girlfriend, I let her know I am just "checking in." She will tell me frequently that "she doesn't want to talk about it." I appreciate her honesty because it sets the stage for the kind of conversation she does want to have.

- Be in charge of picking up donated food and returning the containers to the owners, or organize a schedule of volunteers to deliver meals as needed. Encourage the volunteers to use disposable containers when possible.

- Record the names of the people who donated flowers, either at the home, church, or funeral home. Specify what kind of floral arrangement was given. This service makes it easier to recognize the contribution with messages of appreciation after the services.

The following are suggestions for keeping in touch on a regular basis through a monthly luncheon. This may include one or more widows. It is ideal if you can find a group of women who like one another's company and enjoy the time spent together.

- Have the luncheon on the same day of each month, for example, every third Monday. A set day and time works best. The women know how and what to plan.

- Pick up each woman and take her to the gathering place.

- Allow enough time during and after lunch for visiting.

- Serve "girl" food for a fun time. Take precautions and consider if there are food allergies. I consider girl food to include a lot of chocolate and/or the favorite foods of the women who attend the luncheon. Usually it's a lighter fare such as fish, salads, or gourmet foods, which families don't particularly enjoy.

- Call ahead to remind your guests of the date and time.

- Timing is everything with this loss. If you feel so inclined, don't neglect to try a yummy chocolate delight followed by a humorous movie every now and then! If it is a gentleman you are befriending, perhaps a warm pie and war or action movie would be more appropriate, depending on his interests. Of course, humorous movies are great tonics for anyone!

Chapter 8

Putting the "Gentle" Back in the Man

When I was twenty-six I had the good fortune to work with Max. He was my boss, and his motto was, "This is how your job is done; this is how I like things run." During this learning curve of understanding my responsibilities, I was also taught with much firmness ("And there will be no discussing it, Terri") that Max expected to familiarize me in the ways of gentlemanly behavior toward a woman by his example.

Growing up in the '60s and '70s, I learned the philosophy of feminism and was schooled in the inequality between men and women regarding a number of issues. These topics were regular headlines, along with civil rights, Woodstock, and the Vietnam War. During this time of social and philosophical upheaval, some of the previous generations' ways of thinking were appropriately discarded. These included such issues as "children should be seen and not heard" or families never discussing skeletons in the closets. Equality issues between men and women such as workplace benefits, wages, and the right to work outside of the home were also brought to the table. There were a myriad of points of debate on numerous subjects that caused people to question the way things had always been done before.

I believe that my generation, in this era of free and open thinking, introduced a more informal approach to societal interactions between the sexes. There also seemed to be a movement toward increased familiarity between the generations. There were fewer children addressing their elders as "Mr." or "Mrs. Smith." There was noticeably less politeness with and respect for authority figures.

The attitude of free love and the antiestablishment mentality reigned supreme. Woodstock was one of those "wow" experiences. I remember thinking at the time that it was an event that had significant impact on our society. It was a place of opportunity for my generation to set aside conventional rules of behavior. Many people displayed such casual, even reckless, interaction with one another in public as had not ever before been witnessed. This lax attitude continues today.

These social voices were persistent and loud. The constant current of these attitudes permeated my education and shaped my psyche. At the same time, I did not live at an economic level that required "Emily Post" behavior. I was blithely clueless that for hundreds and hundreds of years, men actually deferred to women in the social graces! In my mind, it was behavior reserved for the movies, not real life.

Then I met Max. He introduced me to the idea that it is noble and in good taste for men to defer to women in simple and thoughtful ways. He wasn't trumpeting his thoughtfulness to garner attention to himself. He wasn't trying to make some political statement. He was simply applying graciousness and respect for women that his generation had learned. I asked him who his role model was. He said there was no one particular role model. There didn't have to be. The whole of society acted this way. Everywhere men of breeding deferred to women. It was not done as a subservient gesture. It was done out of respect and societal mores.

I recall one day that Max and I were on an errand. As we were walking to his car, he reminded me not to touch the door handle. He said he would open the car door for me, as he had many times before. Between the office door (which he opened for me) and the car door, we were engaged in conversation. Out of habit and an "I can do for myself" attitude, I forgot his reminder and began opening my own door, with Max standing close behind. The door was immediately pushed closed. I received a firm but loving scolding by my fatherly boss. "Didn't I just tell you not to touch the door handle?"

"Yes, you did."

"Well, let me open your door. That is what a gentleman does."

Max considers it an honor to defer to women of all ages and persuasions of feminism. He is undeterred by ruffled feathers of womanly independence. He grew up in the '30s and '40s when courteous behavior to women was the generally accepted fashion. His belief is that we should allow men to be gentlemen.

Unless you live in circles where Emily Post and Miss Manners' philosophies are required behavior from the cradle to the grave, the generations of children from the '60s to our current time have not been exposed to regular, everyday, common courtesies displayed from men to women. Nor are women taught to graciously expect and receive it.

There are exceptions, of course, but as a general rule there seems to be a lack of awareness about manners between the sexes. If a man extends a kindness to a woman, such as holding a door open for her, it is often rebuffed, indicating the attitude of "I am capable of opening my own door." Or it is interpreted as being too familiar, with sexual overtones attached. The man can be left confused and offended himself. A look of rejection and a cold response from a woman will simply teach and reinforce men that the common courtesies offered are unwanted. This results in fewer attempts at politeness, and a quandary about roles of behavior and exactly what manners are appropriate between the sexes.

Of course there are always men who are exceptions to the general rule I am implying here. There are men who have developed this sensitivity and consistently behave in a mannerly way to all women. Many women are also comfortable with expecting this quality of behavior from men. My husband was taught to honor women. He reflects his early training with courtesies he extends to me and all women he encounters. Due to his constant and consistent manners toward me, I have developed a confidence in the feminine part of my personality and value the growth because I have not experienced these feelings in the past. I consider it a great honor to receive his courtesies as well as extend my own courtesies to him. A higher level of respect exists between us because of these behaviors. I have come a long way since my days with Max.

It is my attempt to reassure that common courtesies between the sexes are a gift of self to give as a man and to accept as a woman. I offer the following list of suggestions to aid in raising our awareness of "nicety necessities." These can easily be taught and put into one's lifestyle.

As a gentleman, be aware of the opportunities to be courteous to women. There are many chances in your day-to-day activities to take advantage of displaying gentlemanly manners. Determine to make it a part of who you are. As a woman, allow men to treat you with respect by letting them act on their inclination to be gentlemen. Resist the urge to judge, to be indifferent, or to misinterpret their actions. It is permissible (and ennobling) to allow these courtesies to become a natural part of our interactions.

Civil, courteous behavior between the sexes is the focus here. Of course there are inappropriate, offensive, intrusive, and even criminal behaviors, which should not be tolerated. However, in our haste to make sure nothing untoward or offensive is even implied, we have allowed proper etiquette to be diminished. Our children need to model and experience proper manners. This creates a feeling of civility in them, which in turn will contribute to an elevation of general goodness and kindness in the world.

With practice, these kindnesses and courtesies can turn

into habit. You will begin to be more comfortable giving and receiving them. These courtesies will bring out the higher and better characteristics of our beings. They will increase the refinement of our natures. The kindness and manners extended to men and women will help reduce the unfortunate competition that exists between the sexes. Men, try any of these recommendations:

- Open any and all doors—a car, the house, the workplace, a restaurant, the hospital, etc.

- Help a woman put on her coat or sweater as well as help her to remove it.

- It is a rare thing to see a man tipping his hat to a woman these days, simply because the only hats men wear are baseball hats. I doubt very much if they will be tipping their baseball hats any time soon. However, some of the older generation still wear hats occasionally, and you may see them tipping or even doffing their hat to a lady. It's a nice gesture of respect that will soon slip into a societal custom of yesteryear.

- Retrieve a grocery cart for a woman if you happen to be in the shopping cart area. Wal-Mart gives customers a nice service. Many of their male door greeters offer shopping carts to customers entering the store.

- Be aware of automobile needs. Changing tires is a big deal to a woman. Tires are heavy, dirty, and, let's admit it, a big fingernail breaker! Some women know how to change a tire, but the reality of it is that the task is difficult if you are not dressed appropriately, have children needing attention, or haven't adequate strength.

Some months ago, after playing tennis, I returned to my truck at the gym parking lot to discover that my back tire was flat! I know how to change a tire, but I simply did not have the muscle to get the lug nuts loose, lift the heavy tire off, and put on the spare tire. I went back inside the gym to recruit a young stud to help with the tire task. His boss, a woman, was hard to persuade. The young man pleaded my case. I overheard her say to him, "I don't pay you to help change tires." He was persistent, reassuring her it would only take him ten minutes. She allowed him to help me but wasn't very happy about it. Of course, I was very grateful for his help. He did indeed accomplish the task in about ten to fifteen minutes.

Shortly after that incident I did not see him working there anymore. It was a sad reminder of how cold our society can be! I have since thanked the manager for his help, but I believe it was too late to help save this young man's job.

- Hold the chair for the woman as she is seating herself in meetings, the restaurant, and other public places.

- Allow her to enter the aisle of the movie theater first while choosing a location to sit. (Hopefully she'll be sensitive to where the gentleman likes to sit.)

- Wait for her after leaving a social situation. Don't walk ahead of her. Escorting her as an equal is respectful and gentlemanly.

- While descending or ascending stairs, gently steady her by holding her hand or elbow if there is enough room.

- Let her take your arm when escorting her to functions.

- Offer to get her a refreshment or beverage.

- When in traffic, under crowded conditions, allow the woman to pull in front of you. It really isn't a competition. No one has to be in front of the pack. A little civility amidst all the road rage helps to reduce tension and anger between strangers. Of course, this holds true for women to be gracious to men also.

- Because men are built with more muscle mass than women, be aware of appropriate physical tasks that may need a man's helping hand. Some situations, activities, or tasks are too heavy or difficult for a woman to handle. For example, one day Max was working at his commercial building during renovation, and he happened to be watching a woman attempting to back up her car. She would rev the engine, but nothing happened. She tried doing this several times. As Max became more curious about why the car was going nowhere, despite enough engine power, he noticed her front tires were lodged over the cement guard. Obviously, she did not have the physical strength to lift her car off the guard. Max called a couple of other men over to offer assistance, and the recruited team of gentlemen took care of her problem in a couple of minutes.

- Men like chocolate too! Warm their hearts with a great chocolate treat and a guy movie that would satisfy their interests.

These are a few suggestions that may help men and women begin to implement graciousness in their behavior toward one another. Initially it may be uncomfortable. However, if allowed and practiced, it will do a lot to restore a man's confidence and masculinity and develop a woman's softness. Thoughtful and considerate interactions will promote gentility and refinement in humankind. It promotes gentleness and kind behavior. Go ahead, give it a try!

Chapter 8

From Local to Global

This book has attempted to offer enlightenment regarding simple acts of kindness and gifts from the heart on a one-to-one basis. However, during the research of this project I became familiar with women who represent another facet of serving others. I realized I needed to bring attention to their efforts because the work they are doing has such impact. It has permanently changed their own lives as well as the volunteers who work within the organizations they have built. The communities that their projects target are profoundly affected for good by their efforts and are given hope for a brighter future. It would be difficult to judge which group of people are affected and transformed the most.

The women I write about are women like you and me. Each of them has taken a simple idea and combined it with determination, creativity, and passion. This has resulted in developing an organization that effectively nurtures relationships, heals hearts, and mends lives. They wanted to make a difference on a larger scale. I know there are perhaps hundreds or thousands of women just like these three individuals who have moved forward with a yearning to impact and change lives around the world. These examples might give one woman the courage and motivation to act on her desire to make a similar impact. I highlight these selfless women as great examples of what one person can do.

Perhaps you are an individual who would like to create a nonprofit group that focuses on service outside of your local community. You may connect with these women's visions and missions. Their stories are inspirational. They have impressive ambition and passion, which propels them to accomplish their goals. They are ordinary individuals bringing about extraordinary change. These women are Kathy Headlee, founder of Mothers Without Borders; Diana Tacey, founder of ChildLight Foundation for Afghan Children; and Judy Zone, founder of YouthLINC. I introduce them to you with honor. Here are their stories.

Kathy Headlee, Mothers Without Borders

Nurturing and caring for orphaned and vulnerable children as if they were our own.

—Kathy

I met Kathy six years ago at a gathering for women. She gave a brief overview of her organization with the emphasis on current projects. I was impressed with her vision and dedication. I hadn't seen her since, but as I was organizing the chapters for this book, I knew that I needed to include her story, and I knew where I wanted her story to fit. I was fortunate enough to secure an interview with her in spite of her hectic schedule.

Kathy came from a background where she was taught the importance of serving beyond self and giving to the community. She raised her five children with the same awareness and selfless principles. In 1990 she and her family were living in San Diego where access to Tijuana, Mexico, is relatively easy. She drove her children to the orphanages in Tijuana and would engage in small projects, such as bringing toys and clothes for the children or playing with them. During this same time period she would also volunteer her time and services in helping battered women and the homeless in her local community.

Once her children were in school, she volunteered to work with a large humanitarian organization. From nine to three each day she would learn the minutiae that makes a charitable organization function, such as stuffing envelopes, entering data into computers, answering telephones, understanding project development, fundraising, and staffing.

After several months she was asked to take on a leadership role in some of the projects of the humanitarian organization. This leadership role fine-tuned her education in volunteer work. It allowed her to sharpen her ability to organize and pursue projects from start to finish. Kathy's confidence grew as she proved her capability and understanding of the inner workings of the organization. As a result she was asked to sit on the board of directors, a position she held for ten years.

During this time of what Kathy calls "her training

period," she was watching a program on Romanian orphans that "pierced her soul." The content of the show spoke to her, and she said she knew she wanted and needed to do something. Just what that particular something was she didn't have a clue. Eight or nine months passed when a flash of inspiration helped her understand what that something was.

At a family reunion during the summer of 1991, a family counsel was held in which a suggestion was made that every other year the adults take a trip somewhere *sans* children. Kathy knew instinctively that Romania was to be the first destination of the all-adult trip. She also knew that it didn't have the same appeal as Hawaii and that a Romanian service trip might be a hard sell. Eventually everyone who would be able to go came to accept and understand that this choice was the right one.

In the spring of 1992, Kathy and twenty-two family members embarked on their "Family Reunion Service Project." They flew to Romania to assist the medical staff that had also volunteered their time, skills, and means. These magnificent medical specialists had been directed to an orphanage in Romania to correct such physical malformations as cleft palates and clubfeet, in order to help the children become more eligible for adoption. Kathy and her family were also directed there to offer preoperative and postoperative services for these children.

After two-and-a-half weeks of this labor of love, Kathy and her family members were changed for life. They returned to the United States exhausted from the difficulties of serving in a foreign country but with a much keener awareness of how much each person had to offer. Not only did she understand that she had been preparing for just this kind of experience, but also that she would be blessed with the addition of a Romanian child to her personal family! Her brother's family adopted three Romanian children! Their lives were dramatically altered forever.

When word got out about the success of their trip, other family groups asked Kathy to help them organize and execute service trips of their own. This occurred several times a year, giving her an opportunity to fine-tune the process of overseas projects and expand her volunteer work to other areas of need, such as Bolivia and Mexico. She also continued to educate herself in humanitarian efforts by attending helpful conferences.

During the mid 1990s, Kathy was narrowing her focus toward orphans. Much of her work seemed to naturally flow to these motherless and fatherless children. Parallel to this focus she became increasingly aware of peculiar dynamics in two groups of people. First, she realized that the orphan population in the world exploded with the AIDS epidemic becoming pandemic. Second, she noticed that a sector of Americans were getting wealthier much younger. Many of these newly rich people wanted to contribute to the world's needs in ways that would make a difference. It became evident to her that these two groups were a perfect fit, as long as there was an avenue to funnel the funds so that they directly benefit the children in need. Her question then was, "How do I draw these two groups together?"

Drawing from her rich background and experience, she launched the nonprofit organization Mothers Without Borders, organizing projects in Romania, Bolivia, and India, and then centering the organization's efforts in Zambia in the year 2000. Kathy says there are four points of interest that "Mothers Without Borders" emphasizes. First, the organization works with local charities to identify children in need. Her Zambian staff is trained and prepared to receive containers of relief supplies that are distributed directly to the orphans.

Second, Mothers Without Borders goes into Zambian villages to assess the children's needs and evaluate the resources of the village to provide for the children. There is a determination of what is lacking in ways of goods and services. Mothers Without Borders steps in to fill the gap between these two evaluation snapshots.

Third, there is an emphasis and development of American volunteers. Their passion, expertise, and help are crucial to the success of this organization. Teams of twenty volunteers travel several times a year to work on their assigned projects in the countries where MWB is currently working.

And lastly, Kathy has a current project called the Children's Village. MWB recently purchased fifty-five acres of land in Zambia, which will be the site of the first Children's Village. Here the organization will build homes for the orphans that are headed by a husband/wife team. This will give the children a family environment in which to grow and develop a sense of security and confidence. They will be allowed to live in the village until they reach adulthood. They will be strongly encouraged to participate in the village's success in whatever way they can. There will be a trade school for the use of local people to get an education in particular vocations that strengthen the infrastructure of the local community. Kathy's vision is broad, covering such fields as tailoring, brick making, poultry and pig farming, agriculture, gardening, health and hygiene education, HIV education, simple construction, developing a service club, and teaching basic interpersonal skills of cooperation.

There are overwhelming numbers of orphans and children in need in Zambia. As Mothers Without Borders continues to extend their arms of love to these children, their influence and support will aid in stemming the tide of rampant disease and ignorant behavior. The children whose lives they touch will have hope for a future that has some measure of success. What the children do with this opportunity and gift that Mothers Without Borders offers them is, of course, their choice.

Kathy feels that by contributing her part to the ongoing vision of this organization, she is bestowing more goodness in the world, which elevates that cumulative effect of all the goodness that is offered by people worldwide. It is a positive, joyful message! Below is her contact information:

Mothers Without Borders
www.motherswithoutborders.org
mail@motherswithoutborders.org
Office phone: 801–796–5535
125 E. Main St. Suite 402
American Fork, UT 84003

Diana Tacey, Childlight Foundation for Afghan Children

Diana has been a friend of mine since we were eleven years old. She moved to Oregon from southern California, complete with white lipstick, long, straight hair, and tanned skin. She represented the epitome of cool from my young perspective. I was completely enthralled with how she approached life in her relaxed, California way. I observed her over the years, happily entertaining our friends throughout high school or becoming very concerned about and involved in the current social concerns of the times.

When I made a phone call to her several years ago to get caught up with each other's lives, I was not surprised to learn that her catering company was flourishing. She had built it from a desire to entertain and a love of cooking, which talents she now shared with the Mesa, Arizona, community. What I was surprised to find out was that in addition to this very full-time job, she had started a nonprofit organization to help the women and children of Afghanistan. This is her story.

Not long after the terrible events of September 11, 2001, Diana began paying closer attention to the reviews, articles, and reports about Afghanistan. In December 2001 she read an article on the Internet by Kathy Gannon, Islamabad Bureau Chief for the Associated Press. It was called "Kabul's Forgotten Orphans Suffer." Kathy was the only western journalist in Kabul at the time the US bombing occurred and forced the Taliban to flee. The article showed a photo of a little boy at an orphanage looking out of the window. The article had a powerful effect on Diana, and she felt drawn to these children and this part of the world in a way she could not fully explain. Diana contacted Kathy, expressing her desire to do something. She was directed to contact individuals that were very familiar with the situation in Afghanistan. A meeting and phone call with one person led to more contacts and phone calls, until in April 2002 she contacted a woman who suggested that if she was serious about making an impact, she should work with the Abdul Haq Foundation, a nongovernmental organization (NGO) based in Afghanistan. Abdul Haq was this woman's brother, who had been instrumental in repelling the Russian invasion in Afghanistan and had earned the respect of world leaders, such as Ronald Reagan and Margaret Thatcher, as well as local Afghan freedom fighters. Abdul was betrayed at some point while attempting to enlist support from his tribal brothers to side with US and western allies against the Taliban and al Qaeda. He and a nephew were assassinated the day after they were caught and arrested.

In April of 2002, Diana contacted the director of the Abdul Haq Foundation, who was the brother of the late Abdul Haq. He appreciated her interest and desire to help. His first e-mail to her began with, "Thank you for trusting us." He invited her to visit and said he would personally arrange for accommodations and care in Jalalabad and Kabul. He would also introduce her to some of the teachers and principals at some of the schools that needed help, and she could decide for herself where she wanted to work and what she wanted to do.

She chose to call her new organization "ChildLight Foundation for Afghan Children." Diana liked the imagery that children are full of light and that their eyes sparkle with sweetness, hope, and love. She was also inspired by the famous words of William Wordsworth:

> Our birth is but a sleep and a forgetting.
> The soul that rises with us, our life's star,

Hath elsewhere it's setting,
And cometh from afar;
Not in entire forgetfulness,
And not in utter nakedness,
But trailing clouds of glory do we come,
From God, who is our home:
Heaven lies about us in our infancy.[7]

After securing twelve thousand dollars from a fundraiser (that her company catered), she was able to take her first trip to Afghanistan in July 2002. Her father and another male acquaintance went with her as escorts because of the very male-dominated, patriarchal society in which she was going to be traveling. During this first trip she was introduced to the culture, foods, attitudes, beauty, and desperate needs of the area.

She was escorted from Peshawar, Pakistan, through the Kyber Pass, and finally to Jalalabad. Diana was introduced to several possible projects that caught her attention. As her involvement with these people's needs became more extensive, her awareness of other pockets of needs expanded. ChildLight Foundation has since focused on the following projects to improve the lives of the children and people in Afghanistan.

* A school for orphan girls in Jalalabad has been improved by the donation of a variety of schoolbooks. The foundation has arranged for an art workshop to be introduced and conducted at the school. ChildLight Foundation provided art books, pastel chalk, watercolor and oil paints, and other supplies. This developed into a request for an enclosed art and computer room,

which is a current project that will include desks, chairs, computers, a printer, a world map, and a chalkboard.

- A small village about forty-five miles from Jalalabad called Hesarak had an outdoor tent for a school that housed 650 children with very little supplies, no well, and no medical facilities. Over the past four years, ChildLight Foundation has provided six new tents, has dug a well to provide clean drinking water at the school site, and has built a twelve-hundred-square foot school building. The school now contains classrooms and a health-worker office with a desk, a bookcase, books, chairs, and basic medical supplies. The foundation supplements the salary of the female health worker who is also a teacher at the school.

- Diana met the director of a western Kabul school called "Karte Se Day School." This school is well run and operated by the NGO "Children in Crisis of London." Diana's organization supplements their lunchtime feeding program with vegetables, fruit, and occasionally beef and chicken.

- Diana sponsored a fundraiser in Tucson, Arizona, that provided four computers and two printers for a new computer lab at the Nangarhar Medical School in Jalalabad. This medical school trains eight hundred students, and ChildLight Foundation's contributions became the first computers provided for the students. They have also sent *Physician Continuing Medical Education* CDs, workbooks, and a complete set of medical textbooks that were requested from the school on a wide range of medical specialties.

- ChildLight Foundation has developed a boys' youth soccer program at the Jalalabad Boys Orphanage. Equipment and uniforms for two teams were designed and sent with the assistance of a member of the rotary club of Peshawar, Pakistan.

- Diana has since joined Rotary International, and her local rotary club is working in conjunction with ChildLight Foundation to develop four female-operated poultry farms in Jalalabad, all operated by single mothers and widows with the support and assistance of their children and families.

- They are currently working on raising funds of forty-four thousand dollars for construction of a new Jalalabad Public Library.

ChildLight Foundation continues to move forward with their focus on small projects that bring big changes in the lives of the people they help. It is Diana's hope that ChildLight Foundation will be able to help meet some of the needs of the children in the corner of Afghanistan where they are working. She desires to facilitate and encourage greater peace and understanding between our two cultures.

Between 2002–2008 ChildLight Foundation for Afghan Children has raised over $110,000 through fundraisers, grants, and generous donations mostly from individuals in Arizona, California, Utah, Oregon, and Idaho. In addition, an annual humanitarian team accompanies Diana Tacey on each annual visit to Afghanistan, paying for their own air and travel expenses (about $5,000 per person) and also then donates about $500-$1,000 toward one of the ongoing projects in Afghanistan. Over the past eight years over $7,000 has been also donated directly in-country by travel team members.

Diana plans to continue working on several sustainable projects in Afghanistan as the Founder of ChildLight Foundation for Afghan Children, and also now as a member of Rotary International, who have also supported two Rotary Matching Grants in Afghanistan, through support from her own Rotary Club in Mesa, Arizona.

For updated projects and current photos of the most recent trips, go to the foundations' website listed below.

Diana's contact information is:

ChildLight Foundation
www.childlightfoundation.org
E-mail: taceyinmesa@msn.com
Phone: (480) 964–5484
1959 S. Power Rd. #103–245
Mesa, AZ 85206

Judy Zone, YouthLINC

Open the cage and let something fly in.
—Judy

It began with Sara, Judy's daughter. For many years Judy put money away on a monthly basis for Sara to spend as she wanted when she turned eighteen. Judy thought Sara would spend it on college tuition or on a new car. When the time came for Sara to decide what to do with the funds, she surprised her mother with the suggestion that they go on a safari!

Judy and Sara found themselves in an eclectic mix of people in Kenya, including their male guide and a group of women who simply didn't speak to one another. Judy and Sara were hungry for information and knowledge about the local people and their conditions. The guide educated them about the areas in which they would travel. With this information and exposure to an area that obviously needed assistance, Judy came home with the genesis of a plan.

Judy had recently dropped out of a doctoral program and had returned to the public education arena where she had taught secondary school for twenty years. She was left with a space in her life that allowed her to consider what she wanted to do next. Judy witnessed the impact of the safari on her daughter. Sara had put together in her mind the local needs, the international needs, and how horrible it was to live in an underdeveloped country where the civilians had no safety net, no local soup kitchen, no medical clinics, and where the people were starving. These conditions Sara assimilated and understood. Judy clearly saw the impact this trip had on Sara and the character growth that had occurred.

After her safari with Sara, Judy had some months during the summer in which to consider the direction she wanted to take her desire to help and serve the people in Kenya. Being in education for so many years, she developed an appreciation for the potential for service and leadership that young people in America have but usually don't tap into. She knew that if they were given the right informational tools, given the ability to develop leadership skills, and more importantly, given the opportunity to stretch themselves beyond their immediate gratifications, they could make a significant and positive difference in the lives of the people she had met in Kenya.

So YouthLINC was born. She proposed that young people earn sponsorship to offset the costs of expensive international trips through local service and education. She offered sixteen high school students an opportunity to serve in Kenya for a couple of weeks during the summer. She needed twenty-five thousand dollars to fund her first project. She became, as she calls it, a "street beggar." She literally went from business to business explaining her idea of service and the students' involvement. She contacted 250 businesses, soliciting them to invest in the students' humanitarianism. Only one business did not donate funds to her. With expenses covered by the donations of these generous businesses, Judy was able to launch her first trip to Kenya in the summer of the year 2000.

However, this was not the common humanitarian concept of jump on board, fund your trip, and get placed into a service project already developed. Judy's goal was to shape the minds and attitudes of the students in a way that would positively alter the way they felt about helping other humans less fortunate than themselves.

She requires that the student who is interested in working with the YouthLINC organization be willing to give one hundred hours of community service. This works out to be about three or four hours a week from the beginning of the school year until the following summer, prior to going abroad. Also, the student volunteers are required to attend monthly meetings. At these meetings, volunteer mentors' and team leaders explain the goals of the project for each site. These leaders then allow the young people to come up with a working plan for collecting the necessary items that will be taken to the site during the summer. If there is a need for a certain amount of medical supplies, the volunteer figures out how to collect what is needed.

Also, the student volunteers are coached in the skills and knowledge needed for the project. For example, in the tiny village of Yanamono on the Amazon River in Peru, the people were in desperate need of dental care. A group of YouthLINC students learned how to take dental histories and teach dental hygiene so that when the American dentist arrived, the intake exams were already done.

Another need was teaching the young people in Mexico that smoking cigarettes is harmful to their health. The YL volunteers assigned to this project spent time learning information about the short-and long-term effects of smoking. When they went to Mexico, they were put to work educating the local young people with the information they had gained. This is in addition to the one hundred hours of community service work that they do during the year.

The current projects are focusing on three sites: Kenya, Peru, and Mexico. There are approximately twenty to twenty-five youth assigned per site. There are several mentors and team leaders that organize and oversee each site. Judy coordinates the details to ensure that no trips overlap. Once the trip to Kenya is completed, Peru will be launched, and then the trip to Mexico will be initiated.

YouthLINC's aim is to initiate and inspire the young American into the path of service, beginning with service at the local level. If you are interested, contact Judy at:

youthlinc@earthlink.net
www.youthlinc.org
Phone (801) 467–4417
Fax (801) 467–1982
1140 E. Brickyard Rd. Suite #76
Salt Lake City, UT 84106

Chapter 10

"Mankind Is My Business!"

In the classic story *A Christmas Carol,* Ebenezer Scrooge is visited and instructed by his old, dead business partner, Jacob Marley. Ebenezer is introduced to the concept that there must be life outside of one's self. While Scrooge tries to comprehend the specter and his message that is before his eyes, Marley is desperately striving to convey to Scrooge the importance of serving one's fellow man.

> 'Oh! Captive, bound, and double-ironed,' cried the phantom, 'not to know that any Christian spirit working kindly in its little sphere, whatever it may be, will find its mortal life too short for its vast means of usefulness... Not to know that no space of regret can make amends for one life's opportunities misused! Yet such was I! Oh! Such was I!'
>
> 'But you were always a good man of business, Jacob,' faltered Scrooge, who now began to apply this to himself.
>
> 'Business!' cried the Ghost, wringing its hands

again. 'Mankind was my business. The common welfare was my business; charity, mercy, forbearance, and benevolence were all my business. The dealings of my trade were but a drop of water in the comprehensive ocean of my business!'[18]

So Scrooge is given an opportunity for a lifestyle change. This change embraces a chance and hope of escaping Marley's fate of roaming the afterlife fettered in chains. These, he explains, are chains he forged in life "link by link and yard by yard." Scrooge is compelled to view his past, present, and future by three spirits who illuminate and educate his narrow view of mankind. After a night of looking honestly at the results of a life lived from a small, mean, and selfish heart, Scrooge cries for mercy from the last spirit as he is shown his final fate of a cold, forgotten grave with "Ebenezer Scrooge" engraved on the face of the stone.

'Spirit!' he cried, tight clutching at its robe, 'hear me! I am not the man I was. I will not be the man I must have been but for this intercourse... The Spirits of all three shall strive within me. I will not shut out the lessons that they teach. Oh, tell me I may sponge away the writing on this stone!'[19]

In his desperate agony of soul, he collapses on the top of his future grave, thinking all is lost for him, only to find himself in his own bedroom with "all Time before him [as] his own to make amends in!"[20]

Scrooge was better than his word. He became as good a friend, as good a master, and as good a man as the good old city knew, or any other good old city, town, or borough in the good old world. Some people laughed to see the alteration in him, but he let them laugh, and little heeded them; for he was wise enough to know that nothing ever happened on this globe, for good, at which some people did not have their fill of laughter in the outset; and knowing that such as these would be blind any way, he thought it quite as well that they should wrinkle up their eyes in grins, as have the malady in less attractive forms. His own heart laughed: and that was quite enough for him.[21]

Although Ebenezer Scrooge is a fictional character, he represents a good portion of human beings who haven't made the transformation from selfish to selfless. It is inspirational to witness this change in a person. There are thousands of true stories the world over, from culture to culture, that recount examples of uplifting acts of compassion that have buoyed the spirits of the downhearted. Many publications, such as *Reader's Digest*, *Guideposts*, and a myriad of Internet websites, are dedicated to printing positive, warm-hearted, and edifying stories of people serving and helping one another. Exposure to these accounts contributes to restoring our faith in the basic goodness of people.

There is rampant negativity and heartbreak in this world of ours. Television, the internet, magazines, and newspapers convey, ad nauseam, the ugly side of human nature. We are continuously exposed to the disasters that bombard and disrupt our communities, the deceptions of many of our politicians, and the unrealistic and immoral standard of living that Hollywood too often portrays.

This constant exposure to so much negativity subtly affects the attitude we have toward ourselves, the manner in which we approach each day's activities, and how we interact with those who cross our path. It leads to heaviness in our souls. This heaviness manifests itself in attitudes that are bleak, pessimistic, and unenthusiastic. From this unattractive emotional place, the activities and interactions we create result in less than fulfilling exchanges for everyone.

Being surrounded by such negative energy gradually seeps into our souls, which in turn depletes our stores of positivism, causing a fear-based mentality. This fear then triggers in us a suspicion of other peoples' agendas and motives, which feeds our negativity. We develop a genuine lack of interest in anything except our own agendas. We are suspect as to what will be taken from us. So we hoard our time, means, and talents, fearing we could be taken advantage of only to promote someone else's plans. This state of fear and negativity then feeds into the negative energy of a family unit, creating a sense of futility and hopelessness. The hopelessness filters back into the communities as we go about our business, the negativity then permeates the world, and the cycle perpetuates itself.

Interjecting acts of kindness and serving others into this unhealthy cycle of negative energy, attitude, and selfishness is the antidote to the poison that, if left unchecked, rapidly spreads from person to person. One simple act of kindness and love to another human being lifts the spirits of the giver and receiver, contributes to a healthier emotional environment, and spreads hope for a better world. It breaks the nasty cycle of dark, selfish negativity. Think about it. If you anonymously picked up the tab of the person behind you at a tollbooth or at a coffeehouse or a movie theater, you will have spread kindness and surprise, which generates a feeling of pleasure. It may not remain long term with the person, but at some level inside they can't help but be grateful for the anonymous generosity. They may even pass this selfless principle along in their own way.

These positive gestures and acts aid in dispelling fear, despair, and a feeling of hopelessness for the giver and the receiver. If nourished consistently, this refreshing feeling of hope and comfort turns into satisfaction, relief, and gratitude. Nurturing these sensibilities creates a desire to pass along to someone else this same gratifying sensation of goodness. This then inspires more acts of kindness. And the cycle perpetuates itself.

I would encourage each of us to learn from the lessons that Scrooge was taught. We would do well to make mankind more of our business in our busyness. As we engage in good works and charitable acts, we will enlarge our souls while we create and distribute light in a world that is overrun with darkness.

Author's Note

The person who invests the most time studying, researching, and teaching a subject always gains the most out of the experience. So it has been for me. I have benefited immensely from the information I have gathered regarding acts of kindness and serving others. I have gleaned tremendous insight into the absolute need to develop a servant's heart. Learning precise ways to move myself out of my own comfort zone to lift a fellow human being has been of incalculable benefit to my character. I have been enlightened with the knowledge that to extend oneself to others in life-saving actions saves one's own life.

When I had my first child, nothing consumed me as much as the love I felt for him. It was overwhelming to receive such a gift of deep love for another human being. I was unprepared for the abundance and breadth and depth this new quality of love infused in me. It was idyllic, magical, and satisfying. When I was expecting my second child, I was fearful that I would not have the same amount of love for him as I had for my first child. I fretted, worried, and assumed that I lacked the capacity to love two children equally. After my second baby was born, I immediately realized and felt my capacity to love both of these children with the same fierce love, for that love had doubled. When I was expecting my third child, I knew that one of the qualities of a pure love was limitless expansion and that she was already included in my capacity to love my children equally and without measure.

So it is with service and extending acts of kindness. When you offer yourself in this way to another human being, you enlarge your capacity to perpetuate kind acts. But the hidden gift that I did not expect was the desire to continue to offer kindnesses and service. It is a contagious offering. You double and triple your capacity and desire to give. With each offering, your soul expands, increasing your ability to be "the pencil in God's hand," as Mother Teresa referred to herself and her work. We, too, can be effective pencils.

I have come to appreciate the quality of being joyful. This is an inherent state of being. To discover inner joy is to discover one's own true nature. Knowing how to serve others will nourish, sustain, and maintain your joy. Maintaining that joy is the reason to get out of bed in the morning.

I have learned to allow for the magic of stillness. It enhances the healing process as you listen to another's heartache. Stillness is the place where you hear whisperings. These whisperings give guidance and wisdom beyond yourself. The stillness is the lush foundation of the soul, where a quiet, random, and gentle thought can take root and flourish. It is in the stillness that answers come to mend broken hearts. It is in the stillness that we learn how to help when we have no clue about how to begin. It is in the stillness that we are taught divine lessons. There is definitely magic in stillness.

I encourage you to have the boldness and fortitude to step outside of yourself and begin or continue to spread—far and wide—aid, assistance, and love. As you begin each day, make the effort to connect with your higher and better self. Meditate and pray. These simple practices will fine-tune your intentions of good works. Be available in spirit in order to be useful in body.

Go and make a difference in someone's life, big or small! It doesn't matter what it is; just do it! No matter how one's act of service may be received, the real measure of merit and value is the intention behind it. With a clear intention, a pure heart, and focused purpose, your follow-through to serve will reap rewards for your personal growth. You will immediately benefit by increasing your own feeling of self-respect and gratitude!

You are, in fact, not Mother Teresa. Nor would you want to be her. You have unique gifts and unique ways to use them that no one else can duplicate. However, you can emulate Mother Teresa and her simple desire to "love one, one, one." Just do your best, and when you do, you will make a difference!

"...a pencil in God's hand"
—Mother Teresa

A Note about References

Throughout this book I have made reference to several sources that would be of help in a specific category. I had anticipated drafting a list of sources that would be useful to the readers and including them in the back of this book. However, as I began the process of gathering this information, the task became overwhelming and daunting. There were literally 435 million websites listed when I was searching for "support groups." There is so much help available, starting with the Internet as a resource, that I could not do this reference section justice. I feel each source needs to be scrutinized and determined useful by the person doing the searching.

I would encourage each reader to seek out the support group or networks that would be useful for him/her in the individual situations. During my attempt at gathering this information, I realized there are amazing, talented, and willing people who want to help. The Internet is the easiest, most convenient place to begin for help. Local libraries are also a great source for local resources. Federal, state, and local agencies are listed in the front of community telephone books of many government-run resources, which can be very useful.

I encourage readers who feel a need for more support and information regarding their personal situations or crises to find resources and people that will help them feel emotionally safe, understood, and that promote progress on their personal path toward healing and wholeness.

Endnotes

1. Family Circle (April 1980) 61.

2. Reader's Digest Association, *Great Lives, Great Deeds* (New York: The Reader's Digest Association, 1964) 118.

3. James L. Christiansen, *Especially for Mormons,* (Provo: Kellirae Arts, 1973) 334

4. Michael Collopy, *Works of Love are Works of Peace* (San Francisco: Ignatius Press, 1996) 35.

5. Crystal Gromer, "An Etiquette for Grief," *Vogue* (March 1996) 116. Reprinted with permission from the March 1998 *Reader's Digest.*

6. Peggy Post, *Emily Post's Etiquette* (New York: HarperCollins, 2004) 281.

7. Catherine Ponder, *The Dynamic Laws of Prosperity* (Marina del Ray: DeVrss & Co, 1988) 280.

8. Michael Collopy, *Works of Love are Works of Peace* (San Francisco: Ignatius Press, 1996) 101.

9. http://www.visions.ab (website no longer active)

10. http://www.visions.ab(website no longer active)

11. Original 12 steps for alcohol anonymous, http://www-12step.org/versions-of-the-12-Steps.html

12. Article written by Diana Shepherd, "Emotional Rescue," http://www.divorcemagazine.com

13. Managing the Stress of Infertility, "The Emotional Aspects of Infertility," http://www.resolve.org/site/PageServer?pagename=cop_mis_home

14. Coping with Infertility, "Breaking the Cycle of Stress," http://theafa.orglibrary/article_coping_with_infertility

15. Professional and Researchers Quick reference and Fact sheets, http://search.marchofdimes.com/cgi-bin

16. http://hopeexchange.com(website no longer active)

17. Arthur Quiller-Couch ed. 1919, The Oxford Book of English Verse:1250–1900, 536.oDE, "Imitations of Immortality from Recollections of Early Childhood," http://bartleby.com/101/536.html

18. Charles Dickens, *A Christmas Carol* (New York: Gramercy Books, 1982) 243.

19. Ibid. 581.

20. Ibid. 581.

21. Ibid. 585.

listen|imagine|view|experience

AUDIO BOOK DOWNLOAD INCLUDED WITH THIS BOOK!

In your hands you hold a complete digital entertainment package. Besides purchasing the paper version of this book, this book includes a free download of the audio version of this book. Simply use the code listed below when visiting our website. Once downloaded to your computer, you can listen to the book through your computer's speakers, burn it to an audio CD or save the file to your portable music device (such as Apple's popular iPod) and listen on the go!

How to get your free audio book digital download:

1. Visit www.tatepublishing.com and click on the e|LIVE logo on the home page.
2. Enter the following coupon code:
   94f6-ff9e-fe73-1ce6-c26e-8fdf-1966-2bc3
3. Download the audio book from your e|LIVE digital locker and begin enjoying your new digital entertainment package today!